Module C1 — Carbon Chemistry

Module C1 — Carbon Chemistry

Page 1 — Atoms, Molecules and Compounds

Q1 a) electrons
b) nucleus
c) nucleus
d) electrons

Q2 a) false
b) true
c) true
d) true

Q3 a) methane
b) CH_4
c) 4
d) C_2H_6
e) 7
f) C_3H_8
g) 10

Q4 a) C_2H_5OH (accept C_2H_6O)
b) 9

Q5 a) i) O_2
ii) CO_2
iii) H_2SO_4
b) i) one
ii) three
iii) one

Pages 2-3 — Chemical Equations

Q1 a) carbon and oxygen
b) carbon dioxide
c) There are the same number of each type of atom on each side of the equation.

Q2 $2C + O_2 \rightarrow 2CO$

Q3 a) Reactants: methane and oxygen
Products: carbon dioxide and water
b) methane + oxygen → carbon dioxide + water
c) $CH_4 + 2O_2 \rightarrow CO_2 + 2H_2O$

Q4 a) lithium + water → lithium hydroxide + hydrogen
b) $2Li + 2H_2O \rightarrow 2LiOH + H_2$

Q5 a) magnesium carbonate + hydrochloric acid →
magnesium chloride + water + carbon dioxide
b) $MgCO_3 + 2HCl \rightarrow MgCl_2 + H_2O + CO_2$

Q6 a) $CuO + 2 HBr \rightarrow CuBr_2 + H_2O$
b) $H_2 + Br_2 \rightarrow 2 HBr$
c) $2 NaOH + H_2SO_4 \rightarrow Na_2SO_4 + 2 H_2O$

Q7 a) $3 NaOH + AlBr_3 \rightarrow 3 NaBr + Al(OH)_3$
b) $4 Fe + 3 O_2 \rightarrow 2 Fe_2O_3$
c) H–C(H)(H)–H + 2 Cl–Cl → Cl–C(Cl)(Cl)–Cl + 2 H–H
d) $MgO + 2 HNO_3 \rightarrow Mg(NO_3)_2 + H_2O$
e) $CuSO_4 + 2 NaOH \rightarrow Cu(OH)_2 + Na_2SO_4$

Q8 $Na_2CO_3 + H_2SO_4 \rightarrow CO_2 + H_2O + Na_2SO_4$

Page 4 — Emulsifiers

Q1 a) i) A
ii) C
b) i) A is the antioxidant because it has prevented the mixture from going off.
ii) C is the emulsifier because it has prevented the oil and water from separating out.
c) As a control. This provides something to compare other results to and allows you to see what would have happened without an additive.
d) E.g. salad cream, chocolate, ice cream, mayonnaise, margarine and salad dressings such as vinaigrettes.

Q2 a) hydrophobic   hydrophilic

b) Lecithin molecules surround the droplets of oil, with their hydrophilic heads facing out into the water and their hydrophobic tails in the oil droplet. This layer keeps the oil droplets from joining together.

Page 5 — Cooking and Chemical Change

Q1 a) The heat energy from cooking breaks some of the chemical bonds in the protein molecule. The protein molecules then change shape.
b) Denaturing the proteins changes the texture of the food and makes it more edible.
c) irreversible

Q2 cellulose, digest, heat, starch

Q3 a) thermal decomposition
b) i) carbon dioxide
ii) You could bubble the gas through limewater — carbon dioxide turns it cloudy.
c) sodium hydrogen carbonate → sodium carbonate + carbon dioxide + water
d) $2NaHCO_3 \rightarrow Na_2CO_3 + CO_2 + H_2O$

Page 6 — Perfumes

Q1 a) E.g. helps to make sure that a chemical isn't poisonous / is safe to use / won't burn or irritate the skin before it is used on humans.
b) Because of concerns about animal welfare, as testing may cause pain and suffering to the animals.

Q2 a) acid + alcohol → ester + water
b) 1. Put 15 cm³ of ethanoic acid into a 100 cm³ conical flask.
2. Add 15 cm³ of ethanol and a few drops of concentrated sulfuric acid.
3. Warm the flask gently on an electric heating plate for 10 minutes.
4. Turn off the heat.
5. When the flask is cool enough to handle, pour its contents into a 250 cm³ beaker containing 100 cm³ of sodium carbonate solution.
c) The mixture is heated. / Concentrated sulfuric acid is added.
d) To neutralise the solution.

Q3 a) Compound C, because it won't react with sweat or wash off easily, and it evaporates easily so you'll be able to smell it.
b) E.g. test to check the aftershave is non-toxic / does not irritate skin.

Module C1 — Carbon Chemistry

Pages 7-8 — Kinetic Theory and Forces Between Particles

Q1 a) gas
b) solid
c) liquid
d) solid
e) gas
f) gas
g) liquid

Q2 moving, attraction, speeds, quickly, evaporation

Q3 a) weak
b) easy
c) volatility

Q4 As the temperature increases, more liquid particles gain enough energy to overcome the forces of attraction and become gas particles. These can then move about the room and be detected by the nose.

Q5 a) X = (45 + 32 + 36) ÷ 3 = 37.7
Y = (112 + 98 + 103) ÷ 3 = 104.3
Z = (278 + 246 + 243) ÷ 3 = 255.7
b) The liquid must first evaporate and the vapour must diffuse across the room before it can be detected by the volunteers' noses.
c) B — Liquid X is the most volatile chemical.
d) E.g. a test to see if the compound is toxic, a test to see if the compound has a pleasant smell.

Page 9 — Solutions

Q1 a) False
b) True
c) True
d) False
e) True

Q2 a) salt, iodine, gold
b) water, alcohol, mercury
c) brine, tincture, amalgam

Q3 a) 100 g of solvent A dissolves 12.1 g paint
100 ÷ 12.1 = 8.26 g solvent A dissolves 1 g paint
8.26 × 50 = **413 g** solvent A dissolves 50 g paint
b) Solvent C — it dissolves paint nearly as well as solvent A, but it's a lot cheaper.

Q4 B and D should be circled.

Page 10 — Paints and Pigments

Q1 pigment — the substance that gives paint its colour
colloid — tiny particles dispersed in another material
solvent — makes the paint thinner and easy to spread
binding medium — holds pigment particles to a surface

Q2 a) False
b) True
c) True
d) False
e) True

Q3 a) oil-based, water-based
b) solvent
c) something that dissolves oil

Q4 a) E.g. any one from: waterproof, hard-wearing.
b) First the solvent from oil paint evaporates. Then the oil is oxidised by oxygen in the air before it turns solid.

Page 11 — Special Pigments

Q1 a) The pigment will change colour if the food is too hot.
b) The design will change colour/become visible when a hot drink is poured into the mug.

Q2 Phosphorescent pigments — used in emergency exit signs, glow in the dark, used in road signs, absorb and store energy and release it as light
Thermochromic pigments — can become transparent when heated, used in thermometers, can be mixed with acrylic paints to give a wide range of colour changes.

Q3 a) phosphorescent paint
b) Radioactive paint gives off radiation which can be harmful.

Page 12 — Polymers

Q1 a) False
b) True
c) True
d) True

Q2 a) A compound that contains at least one double covalent bond between its carbon atoms.
b) High pressure and a catalyst.

Q3 a)
$$n\begin{pmatrix} H & H \\ | & | \\ C = C \\ | & | \\ H & CH_3 \end{pmatrix} \rightarrow \begin{pmatrix} H & H \\ | & | \\ -C-C- \\ | & | \\ H & CH_3 \end{pmatrix}_n$$
b) polypropene

Q4 a) Ruler 2
b) The forces between the molecules are weaker in ruler 1, which allows the long chains of atoms to slide over one another and to separate more easily.

Page 13 — Polymers and Their Uses

Q1 waterproof, lightweight

Q2

POLYMER	PROPERTIES	USE
polypropene	heat-resistant	kettles
polystyrene foam	thermal insulator	disposable cups
low density polyethene	lightweight	carrier bags
PVC	strong, durable, rigid	window frames

Q3 a) The coating of polyurethane makes the jacket waterproof.
b) The GORE-TEX® jacket, because it is waterproof but it also allows water vapour from sweat to escape, which is more comfortable during exercise.
c) The PTFE film has tiny holes which let water vapour (from sweat) out, but which are too small for big droplets of liquid water (like rain) to get through. It also repels liquid water. The nylon layer is needed to make the PTFE sturdier.

Q4 a) Plastics don't decay, so the landfill sites soon fill up. This is a waste of land and a waste of plastic.
b) Some plastics give off poisonous gases (like hydrogen chloride and hydrogen cyanide) when they are burned.
c) The different types of plastic all have to be separated out before they can be recycled, which is difficult and expensive.

Page 14 — Hydrocarbons — Alkanes

Q1 a) Yes, because it contains atoms of hydrogen and carbon only.
b) C_3H_8
c) Yes, because its molecular formula fits the general formula for an alkane.
(If n = 3, C = n = 3 and H = 2n + 2 = 6 + 2 = 8)
d) Propane

GCSE Chemistry

Exam Board: OCR Gateway

Answer Book

Higher Level

Contents

Module C1 — Carbon Chemistry 3

Module C2 — Chemical Resources 7

Module C3 — Chemical Economics 10

Module C4 — The Periodic Table 13

Module C5 — How Much? 17

Module C6 — Chemistry Out There 20

Published by CGP

ISBN: 978 1 84762 623 3

Groovy website: www.cgpbooks.co.uk

Printed by Elanders Ltd, Newcastle upon Tyne.
Jolly bits of clipart from CorelDRAW®

Based on the classic CGP style created by Richard Parsons.

Text, design, layout and original illustrations © Coordination Group Publications Ltd. (CGP) 2011
All rights reserved.

Module C1 — Carbon Chemistry

Q2 a) i) False
ii) True
iii) True
iv) False
v) True
vi) False
b) i) Four
ii) One
Q3 a) C_5H_{12}
b) C_6H_{14}
c) C_8H_{18}
d) $C_{12}H_{26}$

Page 15 — Hydrocarbons — Alkenes

Q1 a) C_2H_4
b) H₂C=CH₂ (structural formula)
c) Propene
d) H₂C=CH-CH₃ (structural formula)
e) H-C-C-C=C-H or H-C-C=C-C-H (two possible structural formulas for butene)

Q2 a) False
b) True
c) False
d) False
e) True

Q3 a) Add some orange bromine water to each substance in two separate boiling tubes and shake. The bromine water in the boiling tube containing hexane will stay orange and the bromine water in the boiling tube containing hexene will decolourise.
b) An addition reaction takes place. The double bond in the hexene molecule opens up, and the bromine adds to the carbons, creating a colourless dibromo compound.

Pages 16-17 — Fractional Distillation of Crude Oil

Q1 a) B
b) C
Q2 a) mixture
b) hydrocarbons
c) last
d) larger
Q3 [diagram of fractionating column with outputs labelled petrol, kerosene, diesel, oil, bitumen; crude oil input at base]

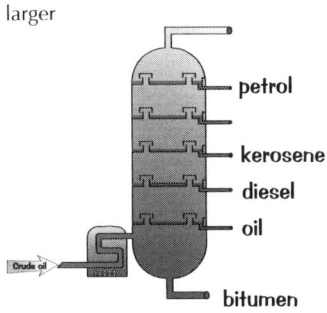

Q4 a) (highest) diesel, kerosene, naphtha, petrol (lowest)
b) (most) diesel, kerosene, naphtha, petrol (least)
c) The more carbon atoms a molecule has, the higher its boiling point is.
Q5 A — heated
B — gases
C — cooler
D — bottom, high
E — smaller
F — fractions

Page 18 — Hydrocarbon Properties — Bonds

Q1 a) Molecules in a liquid have to overcome intermolecular forces to become a gas. Smaller alkanes have weaker intermolecular forces between them, so they turn into gases more easily, and so have lower boiling points.
b) The covalent bonds between the carbon and hydrogen atoms are stronger than the intermolecular forces between the hydrocarbon molecules so they don't break down.
Q2 a) pentane, hexane and decane
b) pentane
c) octadecane
d) pentane

Q3 a)

No. of C atoms	Initial vol. (cm³)	Vol. after 5 hours (cm³)	Vol. lost (cm³)
6	50	8	50 − 8 = 42
10	50	37	50 − 37 = 13
12	50	48	50 − 48 = 2

b) E.g. The temperature that the hydrocarbons are left at. / The size and shape of the evaporating basins that they are left in.
c) The longer the hydrocarbons / the more carbons there are in a hydrocarbon, the less volatile it is.

Pages 19-20 — Cracking

Q1 shorter, petrol, longer, diesel, high, catalyst, molecules, cracking
Q2 a) C — Thermal decomposition
b) B — Energy is needed to break strong covalent bonds.
Q3 a) shorter alkanes and alkenes
b) i) ethene
ii) making polymers
c) 400 °C – 700 °C / high temperatures and the presence of a catalyst e.g. aluminium oxide
Q4 a) decane → octane + ethene
b) $C_{10}H_{22} \rightarrow C_8H_{18} + C_2H_4$
Q5 a) kerosene and bitumen
b) petrol
c) Cracking allows the surplus hydrocarbons (mainly larger molecules) to be broken up into smaller molecules for which there is greater demand.
d) E.g. Cracking also produces alkenes that can be sold to companies for making into plastics.

Page 21 — Use of Fossil Fuels

Q1 energy, non-renewable, increase, more expensive
Q2 a) E.g. any one from: increasing world population, increased demand for energy in developing countries (like India and China).
b) Countries with small reserves of fossil fuels have to rely on other countries for their supply. The countries supplying the oil then have a lot of power over the countries with small reserves and could cut off their supply at any time.

Module C1 — Carbon Chemistry

Q3 slick, waterproof, cold, detergents, toxic

Q4 a)

Fuel	Initial Mass (g)	Final Mass (g)	Mass of Fuel Burnt (g)
A	98	92	**6**
B	102	89	**13**

b) fuel A
c) E.g. any two from: availability, ease of storage, cost, toxicity, ease of use, amount of pollution caused.

Page 22 — Burning Fuels

Q1 a) hydrocarbon + oxygen → carbon dioxide + water
b) i) $CH_4 + 2O_2 \rightarrow CO_2 + 2H_2O$
ii) $C_3H_8 + 5O_2 \rightarrow 3CO_2 + 4H_2O$

Q2 The water pump draws the gases produced through the tube. The water vapour cools and turns back into liquid in the section with the ice, and you can show it's water by checking its boiling point. The limewater turns milky, showing that CO_2 is also produced.

Q3 a) complete combustion
b) i) $2\ C_4H_{10} + \mathbf{9\ O_2} \rightarrow \mathbf{10\ H_2O} + \mathbf{8\ CO}$
ii) $2\ C_4H_{10} + \mathbf{5\ O_2} \rightarrow \mathbf{10\ H_2O} + \mathbf{8\ C}$
c) i) It produces carbon monoxide, which is a poisonous gas.
ii) Less energy is produced than in complete combustion.
iii) The black carbon given off produces sooty marks.

Pages 23-24 — The Evolution of the Atmosphere

Q1 True statements: When the Earth was formed, its surface was molten.
The early atmosphere was mostly made up of gases that had escaped from inside the Earth during volcanic eruptions.

Q2 The percentage of carbon dioxide has decreased by a large amount. This is because it dissolved into the oceans and green plants used it for photosynthesis. In both cases some of this carbon was incorporated into rocks, etc.

Q3 The statements should be in this order (from the top of the timeline):
1. The atmosphere is about four-fifths nitrogen and one fifth oxygen.
2. More complex organisms evolved.
3. Oxygen builds up in the air as plants photosynthesise.
4. Plant life appeared.
5. Water vapour condensed to form oceans.
6. The Earth cooled down slightly. A thin crust formed.
7. The Earth formed. There was lots of volcanic activity.

Q4 a) Largest sector is 'Nitrogen', second largest is 'Oxygen', smallest is 'Carbon dioxide and other gases'.
b) Nitrogen: 78%
Oxygen: 21%
Carbon dioxide: 0.035%
c) There is much more nitrogen and oxygen in today's atmosphere. There is far less carbon dioxide, water vapour and ammonia now. Oxygen is now a significant proportion of the atmosphere.
d) As the planet cooled, the water vapour condensed and formed the oceans.
e) Plants photosynthesised and produced it.
f) E.g. any two from: Killed off early organisms. Allowed more complex organisms to evolve. Created the ozone layer which blocked harmful rays from the Sun.
g) Nitrogen gas (N_2) was put into the atmosphere by denitrifying bacteria and by ammonia reacting with oxygen. N_2 gas isn't very reactive, so wasn't broken down, and its levels gradually increased.

Page 25 — The Carbon Cycle

Q1 a) combustion (burning)
b) photosynthesis
c) respiration / combustion (burning)
d) coal

Q2 E.g. any two from: More people means more respiration; more people need more land, which means less trees and less photosynthesis; more people need more energy, so more fossils fuels are burned.

Q3 E.g. any three from: Only boiled the amount of water he needed/had a cold drink; eaten locally produced food; walked/cycled/used public transport instead of driving; used a more efficient car; worn warm clothes rather than turning on/up heating; gone on a holiday closer to home (using public transport); not left the lights on (or used energy efficient bulbs on timers).

Q4 a) E.g. any two from: The trees removed are often burnt, and burning releases CO_2. Microorganisms feed on dead wood and respire, releasing more CO_2. Cleared ground is used for other purposes (e.g. building more houses or factories, cattle grazing) that produce more CO_2.
b) Fewer trees means less CO_2 is taken out of the atmosphere for photosynthesis.

Page 26 — Air Pollution and Acid Rain

Q1 global warming, sulfuric, nitrogen oxides, nitric

Q2 a) It will react with acid rain and wear away.
b) E.g. any two from: Damage to plants; corrodes metal; acidifies lakes, killing fish.
c) Sunlight reacts with nitrogen oxides in the air to form ozone.

Q3 a) i) carbon monoxide + nitrogen oxide → **nitrogen + carbon dioxide**
ii) $2CO + 2NO \rightarrow \mathbf{N_2} + \mathbf{2CO_2}$
b) Platinum and rhodium
c) It prevents blood carrying oxygen around the body, which can lead to fainting, coma, or even death.

Pages 27-29 — Mixed Questions — Module C1

Q1 a) i) $Na_2CO_3 + CO_2 + H_2O \rightarrow 2\ NaHCO_3$
ii) When sodium hydrogencarbonate is heated it undergoes thermal decomposition and releases carbon dioxide. The release of this gas helps the cake rise.
b) The cake mix is a liquid. Although there is some force of attraction between the particles, they're free to move past each other so the substance flows. The cooked cake is solid and has a definite shape because the particles are held in fixed positions.

Q2 a) cracking
b) It is unsaturated / has a double bond.
c) $n \begin{pmatrix} H & H \\ | & | \\ C=C \\ | & | \\ H & Cl \end{pmatrix} \rightarrow \begin{pmatrix} H & H \\ | & | \\ C-C \\ | & | \\ H & Cl \end{pmatrix}_n$
d) E.g. any two from: waterproof, strong, rigid, durable/corrosion resistant,
e) i) It's not broken down by micro-organisms so it doesn't rot.
ii) So that if it is thrown away it breaks down rather than staying in landfill.

Module C2 — Chemical Resources

Q3 a) The nail varnish molecules are more strongly attracted to one another than they are to the water molecules.
b) The nail varnish remover and nail varnish molecules are more attracted to each other than they are to other molecules of their own type.
c) i) It evaporates easily.
ii) Some of the particles absorb enough energy (e.g. from the warmth of the nail) to overcome the forces of attraction keeping them with the other particles. These then escape as gas particles.
iii) E.g. perfumes. These need to be volatile liquids so that they'll turn into gases easily. They need to become gases so that the particles can move through the air to your nose so you smell them.
Q4 a) Any two from: availability, ease of storage, cost, toxicity, ease of use, pollution caused.
b) i) carbon dioxide and water
ii) carbon dioxide, water, carbon monoxide and carbon
c) blue
Q5 a) i) [Diagram of fractional distillation column with outputs: Refinery gas (bottled gas), Petrol, Naphtha, Kerosene, Diesel, Oil, Bitumen; input: Crude oil]
ii) diesel
iii) It contains larger molecules. There are stronger intermolecular forces between larger molecules, which makes it harder for them to escape as gases.
b) The crude oil mixture is heated until most of it has turned into gas. The gases move up the column, gradually cooling as they do so. Different sized molecules turn back into liquids and drain off at different points.
c) Plastics are mostly manufactured from crude oil. This is a non-renewable resource and will one day run out. As it gets used up, the price will rise, so plastics will become increasingly expensive.
Q6 a) Similarly to Earth's early atmosphere, there is a very high percentage of carbon dioxide and little oxygen and nitrogen.
b) Compared to the Earth's current atmosphere there is a higher percentage of carbon dioxide on Mars, and much less oxygen and nitrogen.
c) Human activity is increasing the amount of carbon dioxide. We're also releasing many polluting gases such as sulfur dioxide, nitrogen oxides and carbon monoxide.

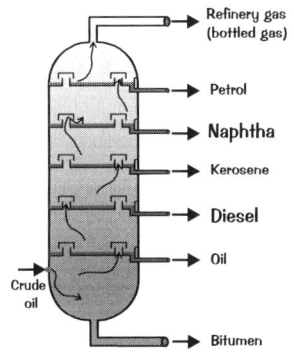

Module C2 — Chemical Resources
Pages 30-31 — The Earth's Structure

Q1 [Diagram of Earth showing crust, mantle, core]

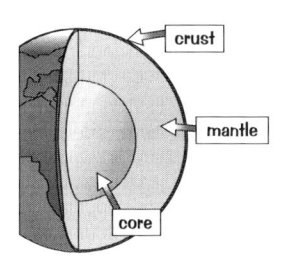

Q2 Lithosphere — The crust and upper mantle, made up of a 'jigsaw' of plates.
Crust — The Earth's thin outer layer of solid rock.
Mantle — A solid section of the Earth between the crust and the core.
Tectonic plates — Large pieces of the lithosphere.
Seismic waves — Shock waves produced by an earthquake or an explosion.
Earthquakes — Caused by sudden movements of plates against each other.
Q3 radioactive, heat, convection, mantle, tectonic, slow.
Q4 a) thick
b) seismic
c) solids
d) outer core, liquid
Q5 a) 1.6 × 10 000 = 16 000 cm = 160 m or 0.16 km
b) 1.6 × 20 000 = 32 000 cm = 0.32 km
0.32 km + 325 km = 325.32 km
Q6 The main earthquake zones are along the plate boundaries.

Page 32 — Plate Tectonics

Q1 a) False
b) True
c) False
d) True
e) True
f) True
Q2 million, Pangaea, continents, tectonics
Q3 E.g. any three from:
Scientists studying the mid-Atlantic ridge discovered that the sea floor was spreading.
The magnetic orientations of rock bands on either side of the mid-Atlantic ridge are symmetrical.
The formation of new mountains suggests that the continents are moving and colliding with each other.
The coastlines of South America and Africa seem to match.
Fossils of identical plants and animals were found on different continents.
Rocks with matching layers have been found on different continents.

Page 33 — Volcanic Eruptions

Q1 1. Continental crust and oceanic crust collide.
2. The denser oceanic crust is forced underground (subduction).
3. Rock melts underground, forming magma.
4. Magma rises up through the dense crust to the surface, forming a volcano.
Q2 a) The lava is runny.
b) Eruptions from volcanoes that produce silica-rich rhyolite are explosive.

Module C2 — Chemical Resources

Q3 a) E.g. any one from: Movement of magma below the ground near to a volcano. Small earthquakes detected near to the volcano.
  b) B — Geologists cannot say for certain that a volcano is about to erupt, but can often tell if an eruption is likely to happen.

Pages 34-35 — The Three Different Types of Rock

Q1 a) igneous rocks — formed when magma cools
metamorphic rocks — formed under intense heat and pressure
sedimentary rocks — formed from layers of sediment
  b) i) e.g. granite
    ii) e.g. limestone
    iii) e.g. marble
Q2 a) E.g. the church is made from limestone which is formed mostly from sea shells.
  b) Pressure forces out water. Fluids flowing through the pores deposit minerals that cement the sediment together.
  c) They are both the same chemical — calcium carbonate.
Q3 sedimentary, heat, texture, metamorphic, magma, igneous, crystals.
Q4 a) 1. Sea creatures die.
    2. Dead sea creatures become buried in sediment.
    3. Several layers of sediment build up and compress the lower layers.
    4. Natural mineral cement sticks the sediment together and limestone forms.
    5. Heat and pressure causes limestone to change into marble.
  b) E.g. limestone is mostly made of crushed seashells cemented together. Marble is made up of small crystals. This gives it a more even texture than limestone and makes it much harder.
  c) granite
Q5 a) Thermal decomposition is when one substance chemically breaks down into at least two new substances when it's heated.
  b) Word equation: calcium carbonate → calcium oxide + carbon dioxide
Symbol equation: $CaCO_3(s) \rightarrow CaO(s) + CO_2(g)$

Page 36 — Construction Materials

Q1 cement — limestone, clay
bricks — clay
iron — ores
aluminium — ores
concrete — limestone, clay, sand, gravel
Q2 a) melting, calcium carbonate, silicon dioxide, sodium carbonate
  b) clay, fired, bricks
  c) clay, cement
Q3 a) It's a combination of steel and concrete.
  b) It combines the hardness of normal concrete with the flexibility and strength of steel.
Q4 E.g. any 3 from: uses up land, destroys habitats, transporting rock causes noise and air pollution, noise of explosives and dust from quarry itself.

Page 37 — Extracting Pure Copper

Q1 a) E.g. by mixing it with carbon and heating.
  b) impure copper
  c) Electrons come off atoms of copper at the anode, giving Cu^{2+} ions. These positive ions are attracted to the (negative) cathode, where they gain electrons. They become copper atoms again, and bind to the cathode increasing its mass.

Q2 A = anode / impure copper
B = Cu^{2+} (ions)
C = copper (II) sulfate solution
D = sludge
E = cathode / pure copper
Q3 a) i) Cathode: $Cu^{2+} + 2e^- \rightarrow Cu$
    ii) Anode: $Cu \rightarrow Cu^{2+} + 2e^-$
  b) A reduction reaction is one where a substance **gains** electrons or **loses** oxygen.
Q4 The following boxes should be ticked:
It's cheaper than mining new copper.
It uses less energy and therefore less fossil fuel.

Pages 38-39 — Alloys

Q1 alloy, non-metal, carbon, brass
Q2 a) i) True
    ii) False
    iii) False
    iv) True
    v) True
    vi) False
    vii) False
  b) Steel — car bodies, cutlery, girders
Bronze — bells, sculptures
Brass — musical instruments, doorknobs
Amalgam — teeth fillings
Nitinol — shape retaining spectacle frames
Q3 a) harder, stronger, more
  b) 90%
  c) Hi-copper bronze
Q4 a) E.g. there would be little time to make the join.
  b) The car body could be returned to its original shape after being dented.
  c) E.g. brass is harder than copper.
  d) Copper and tin would corrode much faster than bronze.
  e) i) Steel is stronger than iron.
    ii) Steel is less likely to rust than iron.

Page 40 — Building Cars

Q1 rusting, iron, water, iron(III) oxide, oxidation, salty
Q2 Steel — advantage: any one of e.g.: reasonably strong, easy to bend into shape (malleable), can be welded together, fairly cheap.
disadvantage: any one of e.g.: fairly heavy, will corrode eventually.
Aluminium — advantage: any one of e.g.: strong, low density, easy to bend into shape (malleable), very resistant to corrosion.
disadvantage: any one of e.g.: expensive, can't be welded together.
Q3 Dashboard — Material: plastic; Advantage: light and hardwearing.
Windows — Material: glass; Advantage: Transparent.
Seats — Material: Natural and synthetic fibres; Advantage: light and hardwearing.
Electrical wiring — Material: Copper; Advantage: Electrical conductor.
Q4 a) True
  b) False (by law, in 2015 95% of the car should be recyclable)
  c) False (it's difficult to sort out the non-metal bits of the car)
  d) True

Module C2 — Chemical Resources

Page 41 — Acids and Bases

Q1 a) An acid is a substance with a pH less than 7 / a substance that forms H⁺ ions in water.
b) A base is a substance with a pH more than 7.
c) An alkali is a base that is soluble in water / a substance that forms OH⁻ ions in water.
Q2 a) Distilled water — pale green — 7 — neutral
b) Rainwater — yellow — 5/6 — weak acid
c) Caustic soda — purple — 14 — strong alkali
d) Washing-up liquid — dark green/blue — 8/9 — weak alkali
e) Car battery acid — red — 1 — strong acid
Q3 a) acid + base → salt + water
b) i) H⁺
ii) OH⁻
iii) OH⁻
iv) H⁺
c) H⁺ + OH⁻ ⇌ H₂O
Q4 a) The pH increases from pH 1 to pH 9.
b) 3

Pages 42-43 — Reactions of Acids

Q1 a) hydrochloric acid + lead oxide → **lead** chloride + water.
b) nitric acid + copper hydroxide → copper **nitrate** + water.
c) sulfuric acid + zinc oxide → zinc sulfate + **water**
d) hydrochloric acid + **nickel** oxide → nickel **chloride** + water
e) **nitric** acid + copper oxide → **copper** nitrate + **water**
f) phosphoric acid + **sodium** hydroxide → sodium **phosphate** + **water**
Q2 a) ii) and iv) should be ticked.
b) The two equations should be:
H₂SO₄ + CuO → CuSO₄ + H₂O and
HCl + NaOH → NaCl + H₂O
Q3 a) NH₃
b) NH₃ + HNO₃ → NH₄NO₃
c) No water is produced.
d) Because it has nitrogen from two sources, the ammonia and the nitric acid.
Q4 a) i) H₂SO₄ + **2KOH** → K₂SO₄ + 2H₂O
ii) 2HNO₃ + CuO → Cu(NO₃)₂ + **H₂O**
iii) **HCl** + KOH → KCl + H₂O
iv) 2HCl + **CuO** → CuCl₂ + H₂O
v) H₂SO₄ + 2NaOH → **Na₂SO₄** + **2H₂O**
b) i) 2NaOH + H₂SO₄ → Na₂SO₄ + 2H₂O
ii) 2NH₃ + H₂SO₄ → (NH₄)₂SO₄
Q5 a) i) phosphoric acid + **copper** carbonate → copper **phosphate** + water + **carbon dioxide**
ii) **nitric** acid + magnesium **carbonate** → **magnesium** nitrate + **water** + carbon dioxide
iii) sulfuric acid + lithium carbonate → **lithium sulfate** + **water** + **carbon dioxide**
b) i) 2HCl + CaCO₃ → CaCl₂ + **H₂O** + CO₂
ii) H₂SO₄ + **Na₂CO₃** → Na₂SO₄ + **H₂O** + **CO₂**
(or H₂SO₄ + **2NaHCO₃** → Na₂SO₄ + **2H₂O** + **2CO₂**)
iii) **2HNO₃** + **CaCO₃** → Ca(NO₃)₂ + H₂O + CO₂
iv) **2HCl** + Na₂CO₃ → **2NaCl** + **H₂O** + **CO₂**

Pages 44-45 — Fertilisers

Q1 essential, growth, phosphorus, previous
Q2 a) 1962
b) 76 kg/hectare
c) It has slowly declined.
Q3 1. Excess fertiliser runs off fields into rivers and streams.
2. The amounts of nitrates and phosphates in the water increase.
3. There is a rapid growth of algae, called an 'algal bloom'.
4. Sunlight to other plants is blocked causing them to die.
5. Aerobic bacteria feed off the dead plants, using up all the oxygen in the water.
6. Fish and other living organisms start to die.
Q4 Fertilisers must be able to dissolve in water before they can be absorbed by plant roots. If the pellets are insoluble then they will not dissolve and the fertiliser cannot be absorbed.
Q5 E.g. use only the required amount of fertiliser; do not apply fertiliser when rain is forecast; do not apply the fertiliser close to streams or rivers.
Q6 a) acid: nitric acid
base: ammonia
b) nitrogen
c) Nitrogen is used in plants to make proteins which are essential for growth.
Q7 a) Fertilisers help to increase crop yield which means we can grow more crops and feed more people. This is important as the population of the world is increasing.
b) As the population increases there will be more demand for food. This means more fertilisers will be needed and demand for ammonia will increase.

Page 46 — Preparing Fertilisers

Q1 a) ammonia, sulfuric acid
b) pipette
c) burette
d) neutralisation
e) methyl orange
f) Slowly add solution A to solution B whilst swirling the flask. Stop when the indicator just changes colour as this shows the end of the reaction.
g) She should not add any indicator.
h) 12.6 cm³
i) Gently heat the solution to evaporate some water. Then leave to dry and crystallise.

Page 47 — The Haber Process

Q1 a) N₂ + 3H₂ ⇌ 2NH₃
b) It's a reversible reaction.
Q2 a) 200 atmospheres, 450 °C.
b) A high pressure favours the forward reaction and gives a good % yield. But if the pressure is too high the reaction will be very expensive.
Q3 a) It will reduce the amount of ammonia formed.
b) To increase the rate of reaction.
c) They are recycled.
Q4 a) It has no effect on % yield.
b) It makes it cheaper to produce. The rate of reaction is increased without an expensive increase in temperature or pressure.

Module C3 — Chemical Economics

Page 48 — Minimising the Cost of Production

Q1 optimum, lowest, rate, yield, sufficient, recycled

Q2 a) Catalysts increase the rate of reaction, so reduce the time and cost to get a particular yield. However the catalyst must be bought in the first place.

b) Recycling the raw materials decreases the production costs as it keeps waste to a minimum and raw materials can be expensive to buy in the first place.

c) Automation decreases the running costs as the number of people involved decreases, so the money spent on wages also decreases. However, it increases the running costs of the machinery involved and machinery has to be bought in the first place.

d) High temperatures generally increase the production costs because they need more energy and the plant will need to cope with harsher conditions. (It may decrease production cost by increasing the yield or reaction rate.)

e) Very high pressure will increase production costs because it costs a lot to manufacture equipment that can withstand very high pressures.

Q3 a) Process A: 3000 ÷ 50 = £60 per g
Process B: 7500 ÷ 250 = £30 per g

b) The cost per gram is a lot lower for Process B.

Page 49 — Salt

Q1 a) False
b) True
c) True
d) True

Q2 a) Using damp litmus paper — chlorine will bleach it.
b) Chlorine and sodium hydroxide.

Q3 a) A — brine
B — Cl_2
C — H_2
D — NaOH

b) Anode: $2Cl^- \rightarrow Cl_2 + 2e^-$
Cathode: $2H^+ + 2e^- \rightarrow H_2$

c) i) anode
ii) cathode

d) So they don't react with either the electrolyte or the products of the electrolysis.

Pages 50-52 — Mixed Questions — Module C2

Q1 a) Layers of sediment are laid down in lakes or seas. The layers get buried under more layers and the water is squeezed out under pressure over millions of years. Minerals are deposited as fluids flow through the sediment.

b) $CaCO_3 \rightarrow CaO + CO_2$

c)

Limestone → (heat with clay) → cement → (add sand, water and gravel) → concrete
Limestone → (heat with sand and sodium carbonate) → glass

Q2 a) H^+
b) i) acidic
ii) alkaline
c) gradual
d) Magnesium hydroxide is alkaline, so it can neutralise the excess acid that causes indigestion.

Q3 a) Ores are minerals we can get useful materials from.
b) brass, bronze
c) The cathode is on the left. The anode is on the right.
d) The electrical supply pulls electrons off copper atoms at the anode, causing them to go into solution as Cu^{2+} ions.
e) the cathode
f) Wiring. It's an excellent electrical conductor.
g) E.g. aluminium, which is used for engine parts because it has a low density and is strong. / Steel, which is used for the car body because it's strong and cheap.
h) Any two from e.g. it's much cheaper to recycle copper than to mine and extract new copper / it saves on the amount of natural resources used / it reduces the amount of material that goes to landfill.

Q4 a) The oceanic plate is forced under the continental plate.
b) As the oceanic plate is forced under the continental plate it melts, forming magma. The hot magma then forces its way to the surface through the dense continental rock and forms the volcano.
c) igneous

Q5 a) Chlorine: PVC, disinfecting water, bleach, solvents
Hydrogen: margarine, ammonia
Sodium hydroxide: soap, bleach
b) E.g. it provides lots of jobs.
c) H^+, OH^-, Na^+, Cl^-
d) i) chlorine
ii) hydrogen

Q6 a) E.g. any four from: price of energy, cost of raw materials, labour costs, plant/equipment costs, rate of production of ammonia.
b) Pressure: A higher pressure increases yield but makes the industrial plant more expensive.
Temperature: A lower temperature would increase yield, but the rate of reaction would be slower.
c) Excess fertiliser is washed / leached into rivers, causing algae to grow excessively. Plants start to die due to lack of light, then bacteria feed on dead plants and use up all the oxygen in the water.
OR Excess fertiliser is washed / leached into rivers causing eutrophication.

Module C3 — Chemical Economics

Page 53 — Energy Transfer in Reactions

Q1 energy, exothermic, heat, an increase, endothermic, heat, a decrease

Q2 a) 29.5 °C – 22 °C = 7.5 °C (accept 7 °C or 8 °C)
b) exothermic

Q3 a) thermal decomposition
b) endothermic
c) exothermic

Q4 a) exothermic
b) A–C, because more energy is released when this bond forms than is taken in when the A–B bond is broken.

Module C3 — Chemical Economics

Page 54 — Measuring the Energy Content of Fuels

Q1 a) Energy transferred = m × c × ΔT
OR Energy transferred = mass of water × specific heat capacity of water (4.2) × temperature change
b) Energy output per gram = energy released ÷ mass of fuel burned (g)

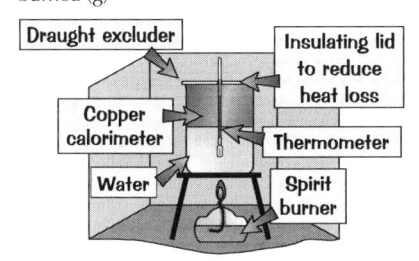

Q2 a) [Diagram: Draught excluder, Insulating lid to reduce heat loss, Copper calorimeter, Thermometer, Water, Spirit burner]

b) E.g. any two of: volume of each fuel; same apparatus — use of lid, material of can, use of draught excluder; mass of water used; distance of spirit burner from can.
c) He could repeat the experiment several times.
d) i) Energy gain = 50 × 4.2 × 30.5 = 6405 J
ii) Energy per gram = 6405 ÷ 0.7 = 9150 J/g = 9.15 kJ/g
e) Energy gain = 50 × 4.2 × 27 = 5670 J
Energy released per gram = 5670 ÷ 0.8
= 7087.5 J/g = 7.09 kJ/g
f) Petrol would make the better fuel because it releases more energy per gram than fuel X does.

Page 55 — Chemical Reaction Rates

Q1 Slow — an apple rotting, oil paint drying, iron rusting
Moderate speed — hair being dyed
Fast — a firework exploding, a match burning
Q2 a) False
b) True
c) True
Q3 E.g. whether they collide and whether they collide with enough energy to react.
Q4 a) i) hydrochloric acid
ii) There is some calcium carbonate powder left, so it can't be the limiting reactant / it is present in excess.
b) It will halve. The amount of product you get is directly proportional to the amount of limiting reactant.

Pages 56-57 — Collision Theory

Q1 increasing the temperature — makes the particles move faster, so they collide more often
decreasing the concentration — means fewer particles of reactant are present, so fewer collisions occur
adding a catalyst — provides a surface for particles to stick to and lowers activation energy
increasing the surface area — means more of a solid reactant will be exposed to particles of the other reactant

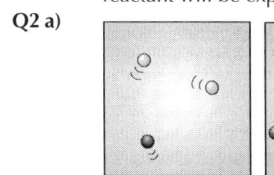

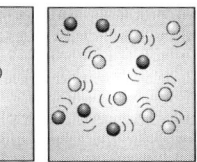

Q2 a) [Diagram: low pressure and high pressure]

b) i) increase
ii) The particles are closer together so they would collide more frequently.

Q3 a) False
b) True
c) False
d) True
e) False
Q4 a) collide
b) more
c) more
d) increases
Q5 faster, increases, energy, successful, speeding up
Q6 Fine powders like custard powder have a very big surface area so they burn very quickly when dispersed in the air. This means they can explode if they come into contact with a spark or flame.
Q7 a) A catalyst is a substance that increases the speed of a reaction without being changed or used up.
b) A very small amount.
c) No (it isn't likely the catalyst will speed up the other reaction) — most catalysts are specific, and will only catalyse particular reactions.

Pages 58-59 — Rate of Reaction Data

Q1 a) i) 0.075 ÷ 5 = 0.015 g/s
ii) 0.023 ÷ 5 = 0.005 g/s
b) B
c) 0.095 g
Q2 a) B
b) i) Curve C should be between curves A and B. It should level off at same height. See below.
ii) Curve D should level off at half the value that the other graphs do. See below.

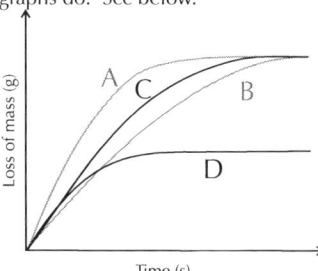

[Graph: Loss of mass (g) vs Time (s) showing curves A, C, B, D]

c) No (you can't tell if it was a fair test) — it doesn't say if Eve kept the temperature or the volume of HCl used constant.

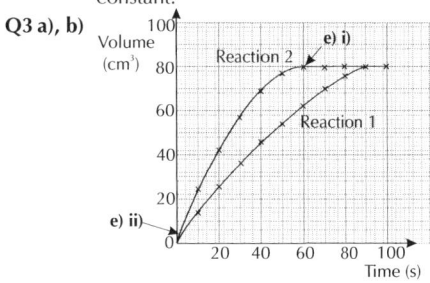

Q3 a), b) [Graph: Volume (cm³) vs Time (s) showing Reaction 1 and Reaction 2]

c) Reaction 2. Its graph is steeper and it levels off first.
d) E.g. he increased the temperature / he increased the concentration of the acid / he used smaller marble chips.
e) i) see above
ii) see above
f) Reaction 1: 25 cm³ ÷ 20 s = 1.25 cm³/s,
Reaction 2: 42 cm³ ÷ 20 s = 2.1 cm³/s.
g) Yes
h) about 30 cm³

Module C3 — Chemical Economics

Page 60 — Reacting Masses

Q1 a) 24
b) 20
c) 16
d) 1
e) 12
f) 63.5
g) 39
h) 40
i) 35.5

Q2 a) (2 × 1) + 16 = 18
b) 1 + 14 + (3 × 16) = 63
c) 14 + (4 × 1) + 14 + (3 × 16) = 80
d) 40 + [14 + (16 × 3)] × 2 = 164

Q3 a) Total M_r of reactants = (2 × 39) + [2 × ((2 × 1) + 16)] = 114
Total M_r of products = [2 × (39 + 16 + 1)] + (2 × 1) = 114
The formula masses of the reactants and products are the same, so mass must be conserved during the reaction.
b) There are the same number and type of each atom in the reactants and in the products. No atoms are created or destroyed during the reaction. Since the atoms on both sides are the same, they must have the same mass.

Q4

Mass of copper / g	Mass of sulfur / g	Mass of copper sulfide / g
63.5	32	**95.5**
31.75	**16**	47.75
3.175	**1.6**	**4.775**

Page 61 — Calculating Masses in Reactions

Q1 a) $2Mg + O_2 \rightarrow 2MgO$
b) 2Mg   2MgO
2 × 24 = 48   2 × (24 + 16) = 80
48 ÷ 48 = 1 g   80 ÷ 48 = 1.67 g
1 × 10 = 10 g   1.67 × 10 = **16.7 g**

Q2 4Na $2Na_2O$
4 × 23 = 92   2 × [(2 × 23) + 16] = 124
92 ÷ 124 = 0.74 g   124 ÷ 124 = 1 g
0.74 × 2 = **1.48 g**   1 × 2 = 2 g

Q3 a) $2Al + Fe_2O_3 \rightarrow Al_2O_3 + 2Fe$
b) Fe_2O_3 2Fe
[(2 × 56) + (3 × 16)] = 160   2 × 56 = 112
160 ÷ 160 = 1 g   112 ÷ 160 = 0.7
1 × 20 = 20 g   0.7 × 20 = **14 g**

Q4 $C_3H_8 + 5O_2 \rightarrow 3CO_2 + 4H_2O$
C_3H_8 CO_2
(3 × 12) + (8 × 1) = 44   3 × (12 + [2 × 16]) = 132
44 ÷ 132 = 0.333 g   132 ÷ 132 = 1 g
0.333 × 1.65 = **0.55 g**   1 × 1.65 = 1.65 g

Page 62 — Atom Economy

Q1 a) copper
b) ([2 × 63.5] ÷ [(2 × 63.5) + 44]) × 100 = 74%
c) 100 − 74 = 26%

Q2 Reactions with a high atom economy create fewer waste products than low atom economy reactions. They also use up less raw material, so they are more sustainable.

Q3 a) Reaction 1
b) Ethanol is the only product of reaction 1, so it must have an atom economy of 100%. (Reaction 2 produces waste CO_2.)

Q4 a) M_r $MgCl_2$ = 24 + (35.5 × 2) = 95
M_r NaCl = 23 + 35.5 = 58.5
A_r Ti = 48
With magnesium: (48 ÷ [(2 × 95) + 48]) × 100 = 20.2%
With sodium: (48 ÷ [(4 × 58.5) + 48]) × 100 = 17%
b) The method with magnesium has the best atom economy.

Page 63 — Percentage Yield

Q1 a) percentage yield = (actual yield ÷ predicted yield) × 100
b) (1.2 ÷ 2.7) × 100 = 44.4%

Q2 a) Using a reaction with a high percentage yield reduces waste and reduces costs.
b) Liquid will evaporate all the time, and more so when heated. This can lead to a loss of reactants/products and a lower yield.

Q3 a) 6 ÷ 15 × 100 = 40%
b) E.g. some of it got left behind in the beaker, some of it got left behind on the first piece of filter paper.

Pages 64-65 — Chemical Production

Q1 a) batch production
b) continuous production
c) continuous production
d) batch production

Q2 a) large-scale, highly automated, consistent
b) Any two of: e.g. It can be expensive to build the plant. / It needs to be run at full capacity to be cost-effective. / It only makes one product.

Q3 a) small, versatile, low, high, quality
b) They are specialist chemicals, so they are complicated to make and there's relatively low demand for them.

Q4 a) Step A: Crush the plant.
Step B: Dissolve it in a suitable solvent.
Step C: Extract the substance using chromatography.
b) Any two from: e.g. to meet legal requirements / to make sure they're safe / to make sure they work.
c) i) Sample 2 because it has the same melting point as the pure sample.
ii) The chromatogram will have only one blob as the drug is pure so no chemicals will separate out from it.

Q5 a) E.g. It needs highly paid scientists to work on the research. Research and development lasts for a long period of time.
b) E.g. It's labour-intensive as the equipment needs to be manually controlled.
It can require expensive raw materials, such as extracts from rare plants.

Pages 66-67 — Allotropes of Carbon

Q1 a) Allotropes are different structural forms of the same element in the same physical state.
b) i) graphite
ii) diamond
iii) fullerene / Buckminster fullerene
c) Any two of: e.g. strong / high melting point / insoluble in water.

Q2 a) E.g. delivering drugs into the body.
b) tiny hollow carbon tubes / tube-shaped fullerenes
c) Nanotubes have a very large surface area. Individual catalyst molecules can be attached to the nanotubes to give a catalyst with a large surface area.

Q3 a) loosely, black, three, high, slide, lubricant
b) As each carbon atom only forms three covalent bonds there are lots of spare electrons, which can carry the electric current.
c) E.g. The layers can be easily rubbed off. It's black.

Q4 a) giant covalent, four, high, hard, cutting tools
b) It doesn't have any free electrons to carry the electric current.
c) Any two of: e.g. lustrous (sparkly) / colourless / clear

Module C4 — The Periodic Table

Pages 68-70 — Mixed Questions — Module C3

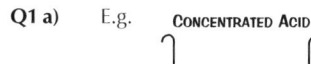

Q1 a) E.g. [diagram of Concentrated Acid container with dots]

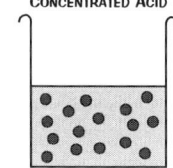

b) The reaction rate will increase because there are more reactant molecules in the same volume. This makes collisions between the reactants more likely.

c) i) and ii) [graph showing amount of product vs time with high concentration curve above low concentration curve]

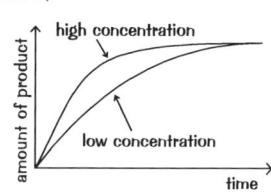

d) Any two from: e.g. volume/amount of acid / amounts of other reactants / temperature / presence or absence of catalyst / surface areas of any solid reactants.

Q2 a) Energy transferred = 100 × 4.2 × 22 = 9240 J
Energy per gram = 9240 ÷ 30 = 308 J/g

b) exothermic

c) The energy released in forming the new bonds.

Q3 a) Q
b) R
c) [graph of Change in mass (g) vs Time (s) with curves R, X, Q, P]

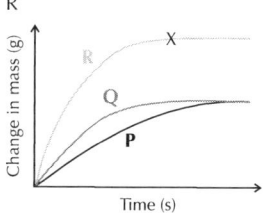

Q4 a) $CaCO_3$ (s) → CaO (s) + CO_2 (g)

b) i) M_r $CaCO_3$ = 40 + 12 + (16 × 3) = 100
ii) M_r CaO = 40 + 16 = 56
iii) M_r CO_2 = 12 + (16 × 2) = 44

c) i) CaO $CaCO_3$
40 + 16 = 56   40 + 12 + (16 × 3) = 100
56 ÷ 56 = 1 g   100 ÷ 56 = 1.79 g
1 × 15 = 15 g   1.79 × 15 = **26.8 g**

ii) [56 ÷ (56 + 44)] × 100 = **56 %**

d) The temperature of the surroundings will fall because the reaction will take in energy from them (in the form of heat).

Q5 a) Nitrogen + Hydrogen → Ammonia
b) $N_2 + 3H_2 → 2NH_3$
c) N_2 $2NH_3$
14 × 2 = 28   2 × [14 + (1 × 3)] = 34
28 ÷ 28 = 1 g   34 ÷ 28 = 1.21 g
1 × 12 = 12 g   1.21 × 12 = **14.57 g**

d) (1.82 g ÷ 14.57 g) × 100 = 12.5 %

e) i) increases
ii) doesn't affect

f) i) E.g. production never stops (so you don't waste time setting it up again) / It runs automatically / The quality of the product is consistent.
ii) E.g. start up costs might be large / It isn't cost-effective to run at less than full capacity.

Module C4 — The Periodic Table

Page 71 — The History of the Atom

Q1 [timeline from beginning of the 19th century to present day with crossed lines matching: J J Thomson's plum pudding model, Bohr's electron shell theory, Dalton's solid spheres, Rutherford's theory of the nuclear atom]

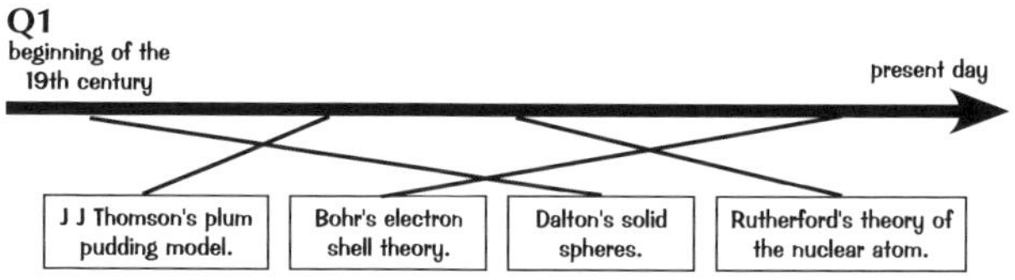

Q2 a) Electrons are contained in fixed orbitals or shells around the nucleus. Each shell has a fixed energy.

b) Because it was supported by experiments / it agreed with scientists' observations.

Q3 a) [diagram of plum pudding model: positively charged pudding with electrons]

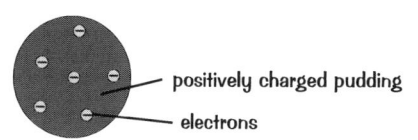

b) Dalton described atoms as solid spheres. J J Thomson found that atoms weren't solid spheres, but must contain even smaller, negatively charged particles (electrons).

Q4 a) They fired positively charged particles at an extremely thin sheet of gold.

b) Most of the particles passed straight through the gold atoms. A small number were deflected backwards.

c) E.g. the results showed that the plum pudding model couldn't be right and suggested that most of the atom is empty space. This led to the theory of the nuclear atom.

Page 72 — Atoms

Q1 a) 0 / zero
b) protons, neutrons (in either order)
c) 10^{-23}
d) protons, electrons (in either order)
e) 10^{-10}

Q2

Particle	Mass	Charge
Proton	1	+1
Neutron	1	0
Electron	0.0005	−1

Q3 a) The total number of protons and neutrons in an atom.
b) The number of protons in an atom.
c)

Element	Symbol	Mass Number	Number of Protons	Number of Electrons	Number of Neutrons
Sodium	Na	23	11	11	12
Oxygen	O	16	8	8	8
Neon	Ne	20	10	10	10
Calcium	Ca	40	20	20	20

Q4 a) & b) $^{12}_{6}C$ (with 12 circled)

c) 6
d) 6
e) 6

Module C4 — The Periodic Table

Page 73 — Elements and Isotopes

Q1 a) radon and krypton
  b) silicon and sodium
  c) sodium
  d) iodine
  e) silicon / iodine
Q2 a) True
  b) False
  c) True
  d) False
  e) True
  f) True
  g) False
Q3 Isotopes, element, protons, neutrons
Q4 W and Y, because these two atoms have the same atomic number but a different mass number.

Page 74 — History of the Periodic Table

Q1 a) false
  b) true
  c) false
Q2 E.g. He chose them based on their properties.
Q3 a) 1
  b) Because he noticed that every eighth element had similar properties.
  c) E.g. he didn't leave gaps for newly discovered elements / he mixed up metals and non-metals / some groups had elements that didn't have similar properties.
Q4 a) germanium, 5.32 g/cm³
  b) 1. The elements each have an atomic number that is one more than the previous one.
  2. The way the elements are arranged matches how the electrons are arranged in the atom.

Pages 75-76 — Electron Shells

Q1 a) i) True
  ii) False
  iii) False
  iv) True
  v) True
  b) ii) The lowest energy levels are always filled first.
  iii) The first shell can hold 2 electrons.
Q2 E.g. The inner most electron shell should be filled first / there should be two electrons in the inner shell;
The outer shell contains too many electrons, it only holds a maximum of 8 electrons.
Q3 a) 2,2
  b) 2,6
  c) 2,8,4
  d) 2,8,8,2
  e) 2,8,3
  f) 2,8,8
Q4 a) period: 3 group: 4
  b) period: 2 group: 2
  c) period: 2 group: 3
  d) period: 3 group: 8
Q5 a) 2,8,7
  b) [diagram of Cl atom]

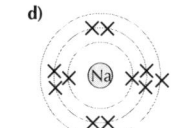

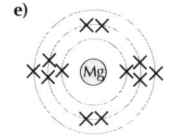

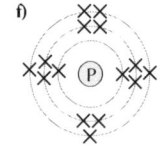

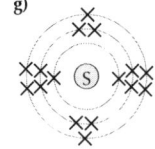

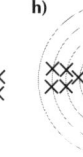

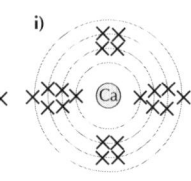

Q6 a) [diagram C] **b)** [diagram N] **c)** [diagram F]
  d) [diagram Na] **e)** [diagram Mg] **f)** [diagram P]
  g) [diagram S] **h)** [diagram K] **i)** [diagram Ca]

Q7 a) potassium / K
  b) silicon / Si

Page 77 — Ionic Bonding

Q1 a) electrons, ions
  b) charged particles
  c) attracted to
Q2 a) A giant ionic lattice / structure.
  b) strong, positive, negative, large
  c) i) lower
  ii) The attraction between ions in magnesium oxide is stronger than it is in sodium chloride. This is because magnesium forms 2+ ions and oxygen forms 2- ions (double the charge of the ions in sodium chloride), and oxide (oxygen) ions are smaller than chloride (chlorine) ions allowing the ions in magnesium oxide to pack closer together. This means more energy is needed to overcome the forces between ions and melt the compound.
Q3 a)

	Conducts electricity?
When solid	No
When dissolved in water	Yes
When molten	Yes

  b) When solid, the ions are unable to move so can't conduct electricity. When dissolved or molten, the ions are free to move and so can conduct electricity.

Page 78 — Ions and Ionic Compounds

Q1 a) True
  b) False
  c) False
  d) True
  e) True
  f) False
  g) True
Q2 BeS, K₂S, BeI₂, KI

Module C4 — The Periodic Table

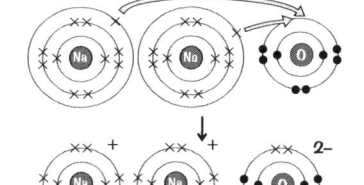

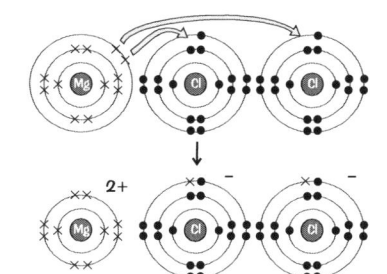

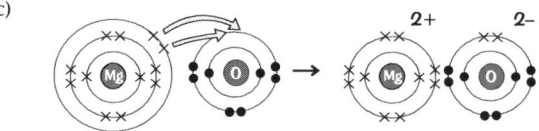

Q3 a) [diagram: Na + Na + O showing electron transfer to form 2Na⁺ and O²⁻]

b) [diagram: Mg + Cl + Cl showing electron transfer to form Mg²⁺ and 2Cl⁻]

c) [diagram: Mg + O showing electron transfer to form Mg²⁺ and O²⁻]

Page 79 — Covalent Bonding

Q1 a) True
b) False
c) True
d) False
e) True

Q2 a) simple
b) strong
c) weak, low
d) doesn't

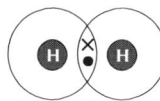

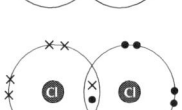

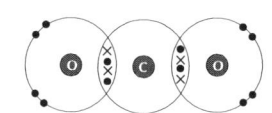

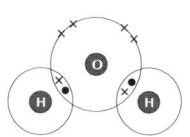

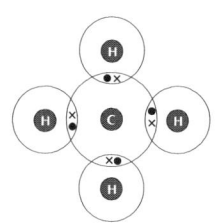

Q3 a) [H–H diagram]
b) [Cl–Cl diagram]
c) [O=C=O diagram]
d) [H₂O diagram]
e) [CH₄ diagram]

Q4 A low boiling point — substances with simple molecular structures have weak intermolecular forces, so the molecules are easily separated from each other.

Pages 80-81 — Group 1 — Alkali Metals

Q1 a) False
b) False
c) True
d) True
e) False
f) True

Q2 a) They are low compared to most other metals.
b) Lower, the melting point decreases going down the group.
c) increases

Q3 a) Lithium is less dense than water.
b) The solution would be strongly alkaline because lithium hydroxide is formed.
c) $2Li + 2H_2O \rightarrow 2LiOH + H_2$
d) i) rubidium + water → rubidium hydroxide + hydrogen
ii) More vigorous — rubidium is more reactive as it's further down the group.

Q4 a) Clean a wire loop in hydrochloric acid and then put it into a powder sample. Hold the loop in a blue Bunsen flame and record the colour of the flame. Repeat for the other two samples. Different alkali metal compounds produce differently coloured flames.
b) i) potassium
ii) sodium
iii) lithium

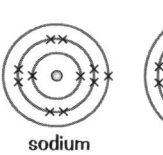

Q5 a) [diagrams of sodium and potassium atoms]

b) i) $Na \rightarrow Na^+ + e^-$
ii) It's oxidation because sodium is losing an electron.
c) They both have one electron in their outermost shell.
d) Potassium's outer electron is further away from the nucleus, so it's more easily lost.

Page 82-83 — Group 7 — Halogens

Q1 chlorine — dense green gas
iodine — dark grey solid
bromine — orange liquid

Q2 a) False
b) True
c) True
d) False

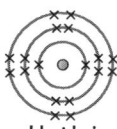

Q3 a) [diagrams of chlorine atom and chloride ion]

b) i) $Cl_2 + 2e^- \rightarrow 2Cl^-$
ii) The process is reduction because the chlorine atoms are gaining electrons.
c) They both have 7 electrons in their outer shell.
d) The electrons in the outer shell in bromine atoms have less attraction to the nucleus because they are further away. This makes it less likely to gain an electron to fill this shell.

Q4 a) sodium bromide
b) $2Na + Br_2 \rightarrow 2NaBr$
c) i) Faster, because iodine is less reactive than bromine.
ii) Slower, because chlorine is more reactive than bromine.

Q5 a) Bromine is more reactive than iodine so it displaces it from the potassium iodide solution. Bromine is less reactive than chlorine so it doesn't displace it from potassium chloride solution.
b) $Br_2 + 2KI \rightarrow I_2 + 2KBr$
c) i) yes
ii) no

Module C4 — The Periodic Table

Pages 84-85 — Metals

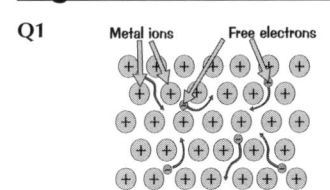

Q1 [Diagram showing metal ions (+) arranged in a lattice with free electrons moving between them]

Q2 a) A, B and D
b) All metals conduct electricity due to the sea of free electrons throughout them. Element C does not conduct electricity, so it can't be a metal.

Q3 Strong attraction between delocalised electrons and close packed positive metal ions.

Q4 Metals contain free electrons which can move through the structure and carry the electrical current.

Q5 a) high
b) strong
c) hammered, malleable

Q6 Metals have high melting points because there is a strong attraction between the delocalised electrons and the closely packed positive ions. These forces need to be overcome in order for the metal to melt, which requires lots of heat.

Q7 a) Metal — steel
Property — it's very strong
b) Metal — aluminium
Property — light / low density / strong / doesn't corrode.
c) Metal — e.g. stainless steel
Property — e.g. doesn't rust / cheap.
d) Metal — copper
Property — excellent conductor of electricity / easily bent.

Page 86 — Superconductors and Transition Metals

Q1 iron — ammonia production
nickel — hydrogenation of alkenes

Q2 in the middle, good, densities, high, colourful, catalysts

Q3 a) The substance with electrical resistance heats up, which means some of the electrical energy is wasted as heat.
b) A superconductor is a material that has little or no electrical resistance.
c) E.g. power cables that transmit electricity without losing power; electromagnets that don't need a constant power source; very fast-working electronic circuits.
d) E.g. the temperatures that the metals have to be cooled to before they superconduct are extremely low, and therefore very expensive to produce.

Q4 a) Because transition metal silicates/crystals are very colourful.
b) You would see green, orange-brown and blue coloured crystals.

Pages 87-88 — Thermal Decomposition and Precipitation

Q1 thermal decomposition — when a substance breaks down into two or more simpler substances when heated
precipitation — where two solutions react and an insoluble solid is formed

Q2 a) There has been a colour change.
b) thermal decomposition
c) copper carbonate → copper oxide + carbon dioxide
d) Bubble the gas through limewater. If the limewater becomes cloudy/milky then the gas is carbon dioxide.

Q3 a) $ZnCO_3 \rightarrow ZnO + CO_2$
b) $FeCO_3 \rightarrow FeO + CO_2$
c) $CuCO_3 \rightarrow CuO + CO_2$
d) $MnCO_3 \rightarrow MnO + CO_2$

Q4 a) precipitation
b) copper hydroxide
c) $CuSO_4 + 2NaOH \rightarrow Cu(OH)_2 + Na_2SO_4$
d) $Cu^{2+} + 2OH^- \rightarrow Cu(OH)_2$

Q5 a)

Compound	Metal Ion	Colour of Precipitate
copper(II) sulfate	Cu^{2+}	blue
iron(II) sulfate	Fe^{2+}	grey/green
iron(III) chloride	Fe^{3+}	orange / brown
copper(II) chloride	Cu^{2+}	blue

b) $CuCl_2 + 2NaOH \rightarrow Cu(OH)_2 + 2NaCl$
c) $Fe^{2+} + 2OH^- \rightarrow Fe(OH)_2$
d) $Fe^{3+} + 3OH^- \rightarrow Fe(OH)_3$
e) You could add sodium hydroxide to an unknown soluble salt and then note the colour of the precipitate formed (if any). This could help to identify or rule out transition metal salts that form hydroxides with distinctive colours.

Page 89 — Water Purity

Q1 a) aquifers
b) E.g. coolant, raw material, solvent

Q2 E.g. water resources are limited and the demand increases each year. It is thought that someday in the future there may not be enough to supply everybody's needs.

Q3 a) 1. Filtration through a wire mesh
2. Filtration through sand beds
3. Sedimentation
4. Chlorination
b) Mesh filtration removes large solids, whilst sand filtration removes smaller solids.
c) E.g. iron sulfate, aluminium sulfate
d) Ammonium nitrate dissolves in water.
e) Chlorine is used to kill bacteria.

Q4 a) Lead compounds from old lead pipes.
b) E.g. Nitrate residues from fertiliser run off. Pesticide residues from spraying too near rivers.

Q5 One from: e.g. it is an energy-intensive process / it's expensive.

Page 90 — Testing Water Purity

Q1 a) A reaction of two chemicals in solution to form an insoluble solid.
b) sodium sulfate + barium chloride → barium sulfate + sodium chloride
c) $Na_2SO_4 + BaCl_2 \rightarrow BaSO_4 + 2NaCl$
d) white

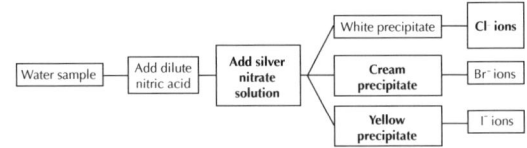

Q2 a) [Flowchart: Water sample → Add dilute nitric acid → Add silver nitrate solution → White precipitate = Cl⁻ ions / Cream precipitate = Br⁻ ions / Yellow precipitate = I⁻ ions]

b) i) $AgNO_3 + KCl \rightarrow AgCl + KNO_3$
ii) $AgNO_3 + NaI \rightarrow AgI + NaNO_3$
iii) $Ag^+ + Br^- \rightarrow AgBr$

Q3 sulfate ions and chloride ions / SO_4^{2-} and Cl^- ions

Module C5 — How Much?

Pages 91-93 — Mixed Questions — Module C4

Q1 a) Isotopes are different atomic forms of the same element (which have the same number of protons, but different numbers of neutrons) / have the same atomic number but different mass number.

b)

isotope	number of protons	number of neutrons	number of electrons
^1H	1	0	1
^2H	1	1	1
^3H	1	2	1

c) i) The atomic number is the number of protons that the atom contains.
ii) All isotopes of an element have the same number of protons and therefore the same atomic number. (The atomic number tells you what element it is.)

Q2 a) [diagram of Li atom]

b) Lithium forms ions by losing its outer electron (to give an ion with a full outer shell and a charge of +1).

c) i) [diagram of F atom]
ii) LiF

d)

Ion	Symbol	Mass Number	Number of Protons	Number of Electrons	Number of Neutrons
Lithium	Li⁺	7	3	2	4
Fluorine	F⁻	19	9	10	10

Q3 a) A and D, because they have properties typical of metals (e.g. high melting point and density, electrical conductivity) and also form coloured compounds.
b) E.g. iron is used as a catalyst in the Haber process for making ammonia / nickel is used as a catalyst in the hydrogenation of alkenes.

Q4 a) E.g. room temperature / 20 °C
b) E.g. so the ideas can be peer reviewed / so other scientists can check for errors / so the results can be used to help other scientists develop their own work.

Q5 a) Solution X is copper(II) sulphate / $CuSO_4$.
b) E.g. nothing happened with $AgNO_3$ so there can't be halide ions present. A white precipitate was formed with $BaCl_2$ so sulfate ions are present. A pale blue precipitate was formed with NaOH which means copper(II) ions are present. Therefore, solution X has to be $CuSO_4$.

Q6 a) Because iodine is a solid at room temperature.
b) $Mg + Cl_2 \rightarrow MgCl_2$
c) ionic bonding
d) [diagram of Mg + Cl + Cl reaction showing electron transfer to form Mg²⁺, Cl⁻, Cl⁻]
e) In solid magnesium chloride, the ions are fixed in place in the giant ionic structure. When molten or aqueous, the ions are separate and free to move, so they can carry electrical current.

Q7 Metals are held together by metallic bonds. These bonds allow the outer electrons to move freely, giving a 'sea' of delocalised electrons. They can carry an electric current by moving.

Q8 a) covalent bonding
b) There are weak intermolecular forces between iodine molecules, so it does not take much energy to separate them.
c) Iodine will not conduct electricity. There are no ions and no free electrons to carry charge.

Module C5 — How Much?

Page 94 — The Mole

Q1 a) mass, relative formula mass
b) i) $(2 \times 12) + (5 \times 1) + 16 + 1 = 46$
ii) $63.5 + [2 \times (16 + 1)] = 97.5$
c) i) $2 \times [1 + 14 + (16 \times 3)] = 126$ g
ii) $0.5 \times [40 + 12 + (16 \times 3)] = 50$ g
iii) $5.4 \times [24 + (2 \times 16 + 1)] = 313.2$ g

Q2 The average mass of an atom of the element compared to the mass of 1/12 of an atom of carbon-12.

Q3 a) number of moles = mass in g ÷ M_r
b) i) $54 \div 27 = 2$ moles
ii) $112 \div [32 + (16 \times 2)] = 1.75$ moles
iii) $198.75 \div (63.5 + 16) = 2.5$ moles

Q4 a) $0.75 \times 24 = 18$ g
b) $0.025 \times 2 \times 35.5 = 1.775$ g

Pages 95-96 — Reacting Masses and Empirical Formulas

Q1 a) M_r of $CuSO_4 = 159.5$
Cu percentage by mass = $(63.5 \div 159.5) \times 100 = 39.8\%$
b) M_r of $C_5H_{10} = 70$
C percentage by mass = $((12 \times 5) \div 70) \times 100 = 85.7\%$
c) M_r of $H_2O = 18$
O percentage by mass = $(16 \div 18) \times 100 = 88.9\%$

Q2 a) percentage by mass = $(5.48 \div 21.92) \times 100 = 25\%$
b) percentage by mass = $(13.44 \div 49.28) \times 100 = 27.3\%$
c) percentage by mass = $(57.6 \div 176.4) \times 100 = 32.7\%$
d) percentage by mass = $(64.35 \div 166.65) \times 100 = 38.6\%$

Q3 moles of NaCl = mass ÷ M_r = $40.95 \div 58.5 = 0.7$
Half the number of moles of $PbCl_2$ produced.
So 0.35 moles of $PbCl_2$ produced.
mass of $PbCl_2$ = moles × M_r = $0.35 \times 278 = 97.3$ g
(Other methods using the ratios of the reacting masses can be used.)

Q4 moles of $CaCl_2$ = mass ÷ M_r = $83.25 \div 111 = 0.75$
Same number of moles of $CaCO_3$ produced.
So 0.75 mole of $CaCO_3$ produced.
mass of $CaCO_3$ = moles × M_r = $0.75 \times 100 = 75$ g
(Other methods using the ratios of the reacting masses can be used.)

Q5 a) CH_2O
b) CH_2
c) P_2O_5

Q6 a) calcium: $20 \div 40 = 0.5$ moles
oxygen: $8 \div 16 = 0.5$ moles
empirical formula = CaO
b) aluminium: $5.4 \div 27 = 0.2$ moles
sulfur: $9.6 \div 32 = 0.3$ moles
empirical formula = Al_2S_3

Module C5 — How Much?

Q7 a) 40%
  b) sulfur: 40 ÷ 32 = 1.25 moles
     oxygen: 60 ÷ 16 = 3.75 moles
     empirical formula = SO_3
Q8 magnesium: 28.6 ÷ 24 = 1.2 moles
    carbon: 14.3 ÷ 12 = 1.2 moles
    oxygen: 57.1 ÷ 16 = 3.6 moles
    empirical formula = $MgCO_3$

Pages 97-99 — Concentration

Q1 a) more, more
  b) no. of moles =
     concentration (mol/dm^3) × volume (dm^3)
  c) i) 0.05 × 2 = 0.1 mol
     ii) 0.25 × 0.5 = 0.125 mol
     iii) 0.55 × 1.75 = 0.9625 mol
  d) 0.25 ÷ 0.2 = 1.25 mol/dm^3
  e) 2 ÷ 1.6 = 1.25 dm^3
Q2 a) conc = 4 ÷ (800 ÷ 1000) = 5 mol/dm^3
  b) conc = 0.69 ÷ (300 ÷ 1000) = 2.3 mol/dm^3
Q3 0.2 ÷ 1 = 0.2. 0.2 × 250 = 50 ml. The scientist would use 50 ml of the 1 mol/dm^3 solution of substance X, and would then need to add 250 − 50 = 200 ml of water.
Q4 M_r KOH = 39 + 16 + 1 = 56
   moles = 5.6 ÷ 56 = 0.1
   So concentration = 0.1 mol/dm^3
   volume = 0.5 ÷ 0.1 = 5 dm^3
Q5 M_r $CuSO_4$ = 63.5 + 32 + (16 × 4) = 159.5
   moles = 223.3 ÷ 159.5 = 1.4
   So concentration = 1.4 mol/dm^3
   volume = 0.7 ÷ 1.4 = 0.5 dm^3
Q6 a) 100 ml = 0.1 dm^3
      0.1 × 0.75 = 0.075 mol
  b) 0.1 ÷ 0.75 = 0.133
     0.133 × 150 = 20 cm^3
     Jared could use 20 cm^3 of the 0.75 mol/dm^3 dipotassium phosphate solution and add 150 − 20 = 130 cm^3 of water.
Q7 0.1 ÷ 2 = 0.05
   0.05 × 200 = 10 cm^3
   Heather could use 10 cm^3 of the 2 mol/dm^3 hydrochloric acid and add 200 − 10 = 190 cm^3 of water.
Q8 a) i) Guideline Daily Amount
      ii) The amounts of nutrients that an average adult should have per day in a healthy diet.
  b) i) 50 × 5 = 250 ml
     ii) 100 ml provides 20%, so 1 ml provides 0.2%
         300 ml provides 0.2 × 300 = 60% of the GDA
  c) 5 × 100 ml = 500 ml
Q9 a) 100 ÷ 150 × 7.5 = 5 litres
  b) 5 litres of stock contains 100 g of stock powder.
     So 5 litres contains 17.6 g of sodium.
     250 ml contains 250 ÷ 5000 × 17.6 g of sodium
     = 0.88 or 0.9 g sodium
  c) M_r NaCl = 23 + 35.5 = 58.5
     58.5 ÷ 23 = 2.543
     2.543 × 17.6 = 44.8 g of sodium chloride
  d) The stock powder might contain other sodium compounds, (e.g. sodium nitrate is often present as a preservative).

Pages 100-102 — Titrations

Q1 Use a pipette and pipette filler to accurately measure a volume of acid/alkali into a conical flask. Add some indicator. Fill a burette with the alkali/acid. Slowly add the alkali/acid to the conical flask whilst swirling the flask. Record the volume of alkali/acid used at the point where the indicator just changes colour.

Q2 a)

Indicator	Colour in strong acid solutions	Colour in strong alkali solutions
phenolphthalein	colourless	pink
litmus	red	blue

  b) It's made from a combination of different indicators, so the colour gradually changes. To detect the end-point of a titration you need a sudden colour change.
Q3 a) To get an idea of where the end-point is — she can then be more careful around this value in subsequent titrations.
  b) titration 3 — 17.6 cm^3
  c) It increases the accuracy of the titration. / It allows you to spot any anomalous results.
  d) average vol. = (15.4 + 15.3 + 15.5) ÷ 3 = 15.4 cm^3
Q4 a) an alkali was added to an acid
  b) By a sudden rapid change in pH / near vertical line.
  c) 20 cm^3
Q5 a) [graph of pH vs volume of acid added (cm^3), showing pH decreasing from ~11 to ~1 with sharp drop near volume 5]
  b) Accept answers between 1.5 and 1.8 cm^3.
  c) Accept answers between 4.7 and 5 cm^3.
Q6 a) 0.1 × 0.01 = 0.001 mol
  b) 0.001 mol
  c) 0.001 ÷ 0.02 = 0.05 mol/dm^3
Q7 a) The dark cola drinks would mask any colour change in the indicator.
  b) Carbon dioxide in water produces carbonic acid which would also react with the alkali.
  c) Kaola
Q8 0.04 × 0.0125 = 0.0005 mol $Ca(OH)_2$
   0.0005 moles H_2SO_4
   0.0005 ÷ 0.025 = 0.02 mol/dm^3
Q9 0.03 × 0.1 = 0.003 mol KOH
   0.003 moles HCl
   0.003 ÷ 0.01 = 0.3 mol/dm^3

Page 103 — Gas Volumes

Q1 a) volume, cm^3
  b) more, 0.1 cm^3
  c) mass, decreases
Q2 a) D
  b) C
  c) A
  d) B
Q3 a) 24 dm^3
  b) i) 0.5 × 24 = 12 dm^3
     ii) 6.25 × 24 = 150 dm^3
  c) i) 0.24 ÷ 24 = 0.01 mol
     ii) 8 ÷ 24 = 0.33 mol

Module C5 — How Much?

Pages 104-105 — Following Reactions

Q1 reaction, new, gas, faster, highest, slower, reactants, limiting

Q2 a) i) 67 s (accept 65-70 s)
   ii) 50 cm³
   iii) 35 cm³
   iv) 15 s
b) The hydrochloric acid (because some magnesium is left when all the acid has been used up).
c) i) 25 cm³
   ii) Not possible to predict. (The magnesium may become the limiting factor.)

Q3 a) 3
b) If you halve the amount of limiting reactant there will be half the amount of reactant particles to take part in the reaction, so half the amount of product is produced.
c) All the limiting reactant gets used up.

Q4

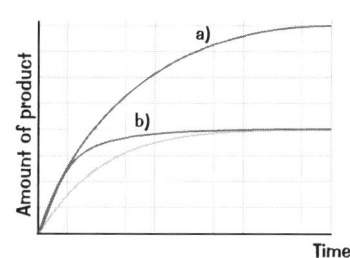

a) The limiting factor has been doubled, so there will be double the amount of product.
b) More concentrated acid will produce a faster reaction, but the same amount of product as there is still the same amount of acid.

Page 106 — Equilibrium

Q1 reversible, products, react, reactants, closed, escape, decrease, concentrations, slower, increase, faster, equal, equilibrium, concentrations

Q2 a) i) A, B
   ii) CD
b) A + B ⇌ CD
c) temperature, pressure, concentration
d) i) The concentration of the reactants will be **higher** than the concentration of the products.
   ii) The concentration of the reactants will be **lower** than the concentration of the products.
   iii) The concentration of the reactants and the products will be **the same**.

Pages 107-108 — Changing Equilibrium

Q1 a) C
b) A
c) B

Q2 a) i) right
   ii) left
   iii) right
   iv) left
b) The amount of reactants will increase.

Q3 a) It increases.
b) It decreases.
c) As the temperature increases the equilibrium moves in the endothermic direction and the amount of ammonia decreases. This means the production of ammonia is an exothermic reaction.

Q4 a) 2
b) the amount decreases
c) The percentage of ethanol decreases because the equilibrium shifts to the left where there are more moles of gas to try to increase the pressure.

Q5 a) Temperature: As temperature increases, the equilibrium moves left (the endothermic direction).
Pressure: Pressure won't affect the position of equilibrium (because there are an equal number of molecules on both sides).
b) Temperature: As temperature increases, the equilibrium moves left (the endothermic direction). Pressure: As pressure increases, the equilibrium moves left (to give fewer molecules).
c) Temperature: As temperature increases, the equilibrium moves right (the endothermic direction). Pressure: As pressure increases, the equilibrium moves left (to give fewer molecules).
d) Temperature: As temperature increases, the equilibrium moves left (the endothermic direction).
Pressure: As pressure increases, the equilibrium moves right (to give fewer molecules).

Page 109 — The Contact Process

Q1 oxidation, reversible, exothermic, less, left, increases, more, compromise, 450 °C, quickly
Q2 $2SO_2 + O_2 \rightleftharpoons 2SO_3$
Q3 a) As the pressure increases, the amount of sulfur trioxide at equilibrium increases. There are two moles of product compared to three moles of reactants, and the increase in pressure causes the equilibrium to shift in the direction of fewer molecules.
b) Increasing the pressure is expensive.
The equilibrium is already well over to the right so the extra cost is not necessary.
Q4 a) V_2O_5/vanadium pentoxide
b) i) The catalyst will increase the rate of reaction.
ii) The catalyst will have no effect on the position of the equilibrium.

Pages 110-112 — Strong and Weak Acids

Q1 a) False
b) True
c) False
d) True
e) False

Q2 a) i) hydrogen
   ii) carbon dioxide
b) i) faster
   ii) Strong acids are fully ionised, so the hydrogen ions are all in solution ready to react. Weak acids ionise only very slightly, so there are few hydrogen ions present in the solution at any one time.

Q3

Name	Equation	Strong / Weak
Nitric acid	$HNO_3 \rightarrow NO_3^- + H^+$	Strong
Benzoic acid	$C_6H_5COOH \rightleftharpoons C_6H_5COO^- + H^+$	Weak
Hydrobromic acid	$HBr \rightarrow Br^- + H^+$	Strong
Formic acid	$HCOOH \rightleftharpoons HCOO^- + H^+$	Weak

Q4 a) and b)

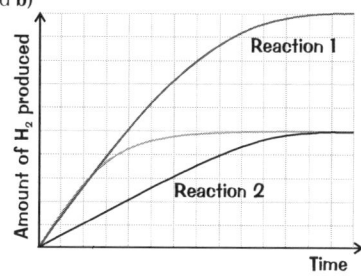

Module C6 — Chemistry Out There

Q5 Acid strength tells you the proportion of acid molecules that ionise in solution. Concentration measures how many moles of acid there are in 1 dm³ of water.

Q6 a) $HCl \rightarrow H^+ + Cl^-$
b) $CH_3COOH \rightleftharpoons H^+ + CH_3COO^-$

Q7 a) The reaction with hydrochloric acid should have produced more gas.
b) Both reactions should have produced the same amount of gas.

Q8 a) Nitric acid, because it is a strong acid and will fully ionise in water. Ethanoic acid is a weak acid so it does not fully ionise in water.
b) There are fewer H^+ ions in the ethanoic acid solution than in the nitric acid solution. This means there are fewer collisions between the reactants and so the reaction is slower.

Q9 a) pH is a measure of how many H^+ ions there are in a solution. Nitric acid ionises completely so it will have a higher concentration of H^+ ions, and therefore a lower pH.
b) Hydrochloric acid ionises completely, so it has a greater concentration of ions than ethanoic acid. The more ions available, the greater the current that can be carried.
c) In weak acids only a small number of hydrogen ions are in solution, but as they react their concentration decreases and the equilibrium moves to release more hydrogen ions. Eventually all the weak acid ionises, so the same amount of product is formed.
d) Both hydrochloric acid and ethanoic acid release H^+ ions so both acids produce hydrogen.

Page 113 — Precipitation Reactions

Q1 a) $BaSO_4$, s
b) potassium, not involved
c) precipitate out
d) fast, large

Q2

Halide ion	Ionic equation	Colour of precipitate
Cl⁻	Pb^{2+} (aq) + 2Cl⁻ (aq) → $PbCl_2$ (s)	white
I⁻	Pb^{2+} (aq) + 2I⁻ (aq) → PbI_2 (s)	yellow
Br⁻	Pb^{2+} (aq) + 2Br⁻ (aq) → $PbBr_2$ (s)	cream

Q3 a) Dissolve the sample in water. Add dilute hydrochloric acid followed by barium chloride solution and look for a precipitate.
b) A white precipitate forms.
c) barium chloride + magnesium sulfate → barium sulfate + magnesium chloride

Q4 Most precipitation reactions involve ions. The ions need to be in solution so they can move about so that they can collide and react with each other.

Page 114 — Preparing Insoluble Salts

Q1 a) B
b) lead iodide

Q2 a) Distilled water — tap water may already contain ions which could contaminate the precipitate.
b) $Ba(NO_3)_2$ (aq) + $CuSO_4$ (aq) → $BaSO_4$ (s) + $Cu(NO_3)_2$ (aq)
c) E.g. Stage 1. Mix the two solutions in a small beaker — the salt should precipitate out.
Stage 2. Filter out the precipitate by pouring the solution through a piece of filter paper. Rinse the beaker with distilled water to make sure no precipitate is left behind.
Stage 3. Rinse the filter paper with distilled water to wash away any soluble salts. Then scrape the precipitate onto a fresh piece of filter paper and allow to dry.

Pages 115-117 — Mixed Questions — Module C5

Q1 a) chromium: 5.2 ÷ 52 = 0.1
oxygen: 2.4 ÷ 16 = 0.15
empirical formula = Cr_2O_3
b) chromium: 52 ÷ 52 = 1
oxygen: 48 ÷ 16 = 3
empirical formula = CrO_3

Q2 a) $2SO_2 + O_2 \rightleftharpoons 2SO_3$
b) i) exothermic
ii) lower temperatures
c) i) three moles of reactant
ii) high pressure
d) i) 450 °C and atmospheric pressure
ii) The reaction conditions are a compromise between a high yield and a high rate of reaction. Reducing the temperature increases the yield, but slows the reaction down. Increasing the pressure would increase the yield, but it is expensive.

Q3 a) Add dilute nitric acid followed by lead nitrate, and look for a coloured precipitate.
b) i) bromide ions / Br⁻
ii) Pb^{2+} (aq) + 2Br⁻ (aq) → $PbBr_2$ (s)

Q4 a) 0.12 ÷ 24 = 0.005 moles
b) From equation: 1 mole Mg reacts with 2 moles of HNO_3, so 0.005 × 2 = 0.01 mol HNO_3 present.
0.01 ÷ 0.02 = 0.5 mol/dm³
c) i) 24 + 2 × (14 + (3 × 16)) = 148
ii) 0.005 × 148 = 0.74 g
d) 0.005 × 24 = 0.12 dm³

Q5 a) 0.2 ÷ 2 = 0.1
volume of 2 mol/dm³ HCl = 0.1 × 100 = 10 cm³
volume of distilled water = 100 − 10 = 90 cm³
b) Moles of HCl = 0.2 × 0.015 = 0.003
1 mole of HCl neutralises 1 mole of NaOH.
So, moles of NaOH = 0.003
Concentration of NaOH = 0.003 ÷ 0.022 = 0.14 mol/dm³
c) M_r NaOH = 23 + 16 + 1 = 40
0.14 × 40 = 5.6 g/dm³

Q6 a) carbon dioxide
b) B
c) Line B. Hydrochloric acid is a strong acid, and ethanoic acid is a weak acid. This means hydrochloric acid ionises completely in water, so more H^+ ions are available to react, and a faster reaction occurs.
d) The reaction is reversible so changing the temperature will change the position of the equilibrium. This will change the amount of ionisation and the number of H^+ ions in solution. So the pH will also change.

Q7 a) 0.2 × 2 = 0.4 moles
b) M_r of NaOH = 23 + 16 + 1 = 40
mass = 0.4 × 40 = 16 g
c) 2 × (15.7 ÷ 1000) = 0.0314 moles
NaOH + CH_3COOH → CH_3COONa + H_2O
0.0314 ÷ (25 ÷ 1000) = 1.256 mol/dm³

Module C6 — Chemistry Out There

Pages 118-119 — Redox Reactions

Q1 a) bodium
b) Yes because antium is more reactive than candium, so it displaces candium from the solution.

Q2 oxidation — loss of electrons, addition of oxygen
reduction — gain of electrons, removal of oxygen
oxidising agent — a chemical that accepts electrons and becomes reduced
reducing agent — a chemical that donates electrons and becomes oxidised

Module C6 — Chemistry Out There

Q3 a) magnesium + copper sulfate → magnesium sulfate + copper
b) Mg(s) + CuSO$_4$(aq) → MgSO$_4$(aq) + Cu(s)
c) oxidised
Q4 a) A reaction in which reduction and oxidation both happen.
b) i) zinc
ii) iron
iii) iron
Q5 a) iron
b) chlorine
c) iron
Q6 a) i) magnesium + iron chloride → magnesium chloride + iron
ii) Mg(s) + FeCl$_2$(aq) → MgCl$_2$(aq) + Fe(s)
b) i) magnesium
ii) iron
c) Calcium is more reactive than magnesium.
d) A reaction would take place.

Page 120 — Rusting of Iron

Q1 a) water and oxygen
b) B
c) iron + oxygen + water → hydrated iron(III) oxide
Q2 a) True
b) True
c) False
d) False
e) True
Q3 a) The magnesium is 'sacrificed' to protect the iron — it is more reactive than iron, so will lose electrons in preference to the iron.
b) Galvanising involves coating objects (e.g. steel buckets or iron roofing) in zinc. Zinc is more reactive than iron, so will lose electrons in preference to the iron. It also acts as a barrier.
c) If the tin is scratched it reveals some iron. Iron is more reactive than tin, so it will lose electrons in preference to the tin and it will rust.
Q4 Grease would be best because it is the best method to use on moving parts.

Pages 121-124 — Electrolysis

Q1 dissolved, decompose, creates, electrolyte, electrodes, molecules, discharged
Q2 a) False
b) True
c) False
Q3 a) [diagram of electrolysis cell: hydrogen gas at cathode, chlorine gas at anode, sodium chloride solution]
b) 2Cl$^-$ → Cl$_2$ + 2e$^-$
c) An ionic solid can't be electrolysed because the ions are in fixed positions and can't move. Molten ionic compounds can be electrolysed because the ions can move freely and conduct electricity.

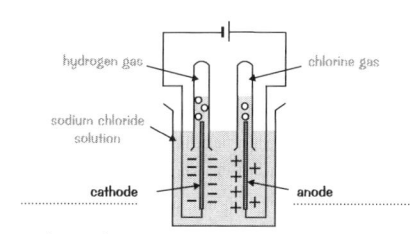

Q4

Ions in molten substance	Product made at cathode	Half Equation	Product made at anode	Half Equation
Na$^+$, Cl$^-$	sodium (Na)	Na$^+$ + e$^-$ → Na	chlorine (Cl$_2$)	2Cl$^-$ → Cl$_2$ + 2e$^-$
Pb^{2+}, Br$^-$	lead (Pb)	Pb^{2+} + 2e$^-$ → Pb	bromine (Br$_2$)	2Br$^-$ → Br$_2$ + 2e$^-$
Mg^{2+}, S^{2-}	magnesium (Mg)	Mg^{2+} + 2e$^-$ → Mg	sulfur (S)	S^{2-} → S + 2e$^-$
Al^{3+}, O^{2-}	aluminium (Al)	Al^{3+} + 3e$^-$ → Al	oxygen (O$_2$)	2O^{2-} → O$_2$ + 4e$^-$

Q5 a) H$^+$, SO$_4^{2-}$, OH$^-$
b) i) H$^+$
ii) 2H$^+$ + 2e$^-$ → H$_2$
c) i) OH$^-$, because hydroxide ions lose electrons more easily than sulfate ions.
ii) 4OH$^-$ → O$_2$ + 2H$_2$O + 4e$^-$
Q6 a) i) oxygen and water
ii) copper
b) i) 4OH$^-$ − 4e$^-$ → O$_2$ + 2H$_2$O
ii) Cu^{2+} + 2e$^-$ → Cu
Q7 a) oxygen
b) 4OH$^-$ → O$_2$ + 2H$_2$O + 4e$^-$
c) water
d) Because hydrogen ions accept electrons more easily than sodium ions.
e) 2H$^+$ + 2e$^-$ → H$_2$
f) i) cathode
ii) anode
Q8 a) By electrolysing the solution for a longer time and by increasing the current.
b) i) 2.5 × 15 = 37.5 C
ii) 0.1 × 30 × 60 = 180 C
c) 4320 ÷ 6 = 720 s
720 ÷ 60 = **12 min**

Q9 a) i)

Experiment number	Current (A)	Time (minutes)	Mass of cathode before experiment (g)	Mass of cathode after experiment (g)	Mass of copper produced (g)
1	0.4	40	5.14	5.46	**0.32**
2	0.6	40	5.46	5.94	**0.48**
3	0.8	40	5.94	6.58	**0.64**
4	1.0	40	6.58	7.30	**0.72**

ii) and b) ii) [graph of mass of copper produced vs current, linear relationship through origin]

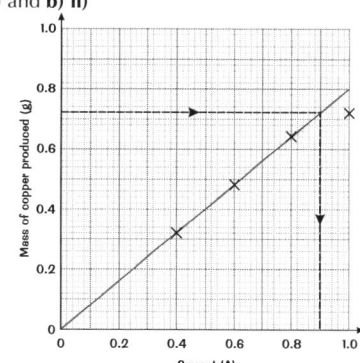

b) i) experiment number 4
ii) From the graph, current used = **0.9 A**
Q10 a) (150 cm^3 ÷ 50) × 80 = **240 cm^3**
b) 1 mole × (240 cm^3 ÷ 24000 cm^3) = **0.01 moles**

Pages 125-126 — Fuel Cells

Q1 a) E.g. [energy level diagram: reactants H$_2$, O$_2$ lower; products H$_2$O higher; labelled H H H H O O at top and H$_2$O H$_2$O at product level]
b) The energy level of the products is higher than the reactants, so the reaction is endothermic.
Q2 a) A = hydrogen, B = oxygen
b) water / water and heat (hot water)
c) reaction, electrical
d) hydrogen + oxygen → water
e) i) O$_2$ + 2H$_2$O + 4e$^-$ → 4OH$^-$
ii) 2OH$^-$ + H$_2$ → 2H$_2$O + 2e$^-$
f) 2H$_2$ + O$_2$ → 2H$_2$O
g) anode, cathode

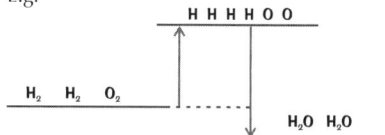

Module C6 — Chemistry Out There

Q3 Fuel cells are more efficient than — batteries or power stations.
In a fuel cell electricity is generated — directly from the reaction.
Fuel cells waste less heat energy — as they use fewer stages.
Fuel cells have no moving parts — so no energy is lost due to friction.
Fuel cells produce only water — so there is no harmful pollution.

Q4 Any three from, e.g. hydrogen and oxygen are readily available from the rocket fuel tanks / the product is water that can be used as drinking water / there are no pollutants to get rid of / they are more practical than solar cells / they are lightweight / they are compact / there are no moving parts that could go wrong.

Q5 a) Fuel cell vehicles don't produce any carbon dioxide emissions (unlike conventional petrol or diesel engines).
b) Producing the hydrogen needed for the fuel cell uses lots of energy. This energy usually comes from burning fossil fuels, which releases carbon dioxide.
c) E.g. hydrogen fuel cells often contain poisonous catalysts, which will need to be disposed of at the end of the fuel cell's life.
d) There is a large amount of hydrogen available for use as a fuel, as it can be obtained by decomposing water.

Pages 127-129 — CFCs and the Ozone Layer

Q1 a) CCl_2F_2
b) chemically inert
c) E.g. coolants in refrigerators / air-conditioning systems, aerosol propellants

Q2 a) True
b) False
c) False
d) True

Q3 a) More UV light from the Sun is able to pass through the atmosphere and reach Earth.
b) E.g. increased risk of sunburn. / Increased risk of skin cancer.

Q4 unreactive, stratosphere, ultraviolet, free radicals, thousands

Q5 a) alkanes and hydrofluorocarbons
b) Hydrofluorocarbons are safe to use because they contain no chlorine.

Q6 a) Diagram 1
b)

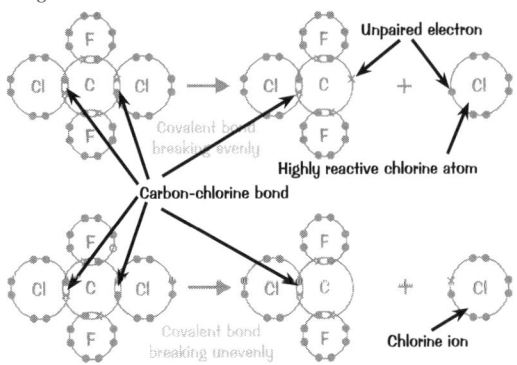

c) $CCl_2F_2 \rightarrow CClF_2\cdot + Cl\cdot$
d) atom

Q7 a) Scientists thought that CFCs were safe because they're unreactive. They don't attack ozone directly, and only cause damage when they break up to form free radicals.
b) CFCs are unreactive and only break up under certain conditions. The CFC molecules already in the atmosphere will stay there for a long time and do a lot of damage.

Q8 a) chlorine
b) decreasing
c) high, were
d) accepted, CFCs

Q9 a) i) Chlorine free radicals react with ozone (O_3), turning it into ordinary oxygen molecules (O_2) and chlorine oxide radicals ($ClO\cdot$).
ii) Chlorine oxide reacts with ozone to make two oxygen molecules and a chlorine free radical.
b) The reaction between chlorine radicals and ozone is a chain reaction. The chlorine radicals aren't used up when they react with ozone molecules, so they can go on to react with other ozone molecules.

Pages 130-131 — Hardness of Water

Q1 a) True
b) False
c) False
d) False
e) True

Q2 a) Ion exchange columns have lots of sodium or hydrogen ions which they exchange for calcium and magnesium ions, removing them from the water.
b) This works for both types of hardness.

Q3 a) calcium carbonate + water + carbon dioxide $\rightarrow$ calcium hydrogencarbonate
b) temporary hardness
c) permanent hardness
d) i) sodium carbonate
ii) Both types of hardness are removed by adding washing soda. The carbonate ions in washing soda join onto the calcium ions in hard water and make an insoluble precipitate of calcium carbonate.

Q4 a) Chalk isn't soluble in water, so there are no Ca^{2+} ions in solution.
b) Carbon dioxide, water and calcium carbonate react to form $Ca(HCO_3)_2$. The $Ca(HCO_3)_2$ is soluble in water, so there are now calcium ions in solution.
c) i) $Ca(HCO_3)_2(aq) \rightarrow CaCO_3(s) + H_2O(l) + CO_2(g)$
ii) The calcium hydrogencarbonate decomposes to form insoluble calcium carbonate.

Q5 a) It acted as a control to compare the other results to.
b) i) Spondovia, Bogglewash
ii) More soap was needed to form a sustainable lather.
c) i) Spondovia
ii) The same amount of soap was needed to form a sustainable lather, even after boiling.

Pages 132-133 — Alcohols

Q1 a) $C_nH_{2n+1}OH$
b)

Alcohol	No. of Carbon Atoms	Molecular Formula	Displayed Formula
Methanol	1	CH_3OH	H-C(H)(H)-O-H
Ethanol	2	C_2H_5OH	H-C(H)(H)-C(H)(H)-O-H
Propanol	3	C_3H_7OH	H-C(H)(H)-C(H)(H)-C(H)(H)-O-H
Butanol	4	C_4H_9OH	H-C(H)(H)-C(H)(H)-C(H)(H)-C(H)(H)-O-H
Pentanol	5	$C_5H_{11}OH$	H-C(H)(H)-C(H)(H)-C(H)(H)-C(H)(H)-C(H)(H)-O-H

Q2 a) The OH group.
b) This shows the molecule's functional OH group.

Module C6 — Chemistry Out There

Q3 a) ethene + water (or steam) → ethanol
b) $C_2H_4 + H_2O \rightarrow C_2H_5OH$
c) Ethene and steam are passed over a heated phosphoric acid catalyst. (The reaction is carried out at 300 °C and 70 atmospheres of pressure.)
Q4 glucose solution, enzymes, temperature, cold, inactive, hot, 25 °C, 50 °C, oxygen, ethanoic acid, distilled
Q5 a) i) glucose → ethanol + carbon dioxide
ii) $C_6H_{12}O_6 \rightarrow 2C_2H_5OH + 2CO_2$
b) i) Fermentation. The sugar used in fermentation is a renewable resource, but ethene comes from crude oil which is not renewable.
ii) Hydration of ethene. In fermentation not all of the atoms in the reactants go into the ethanol, but in hydration they do. / Hydration only has one product (ethanol) and fermentation has two.
iii) Fermentation using a batch process is slow and inefficient but is cheaper. Ethene hydration using a continuous process makes ethanol more quickly. But hydration requires much harsher reaction conditions so is a more expensive process to run.

Pages 134-135 — Fats and Oils

Q1 a) Plants: e.g. walnut oil / olive oil / coconut oil / soya oil
Animals: e.g. lard / whale blubber / ghee / cod liver oil
b) Any two from: e.g. in paints / in machine lubricants / in detergents / in cosmetics / for cooking / making biodiesel / making soaps
Q2 solids, liquids, esters, acids/alcohols, alcohols/acids, fatty, glycerol
Q3 a) It means that they do not mix together.
b) An emulsion is a suspension of two immiscible liquids, e.g. oil droplets in water or water droplets in oil. You have to shake the two liquids together vigorously.
c) Milk — droplets of **oil**
Butter — droplets of **water**
Q4 a) E.g. biodiesel
b) E.g. diesel
c) 37 MJ × (70 ÷ 100) = **25.9 MJ (25 900 000 J)**
Q5 a) Saponification is the process of splitting up fats and oils using sodium hydroxide.
b) Soap is made by — boiling oil or fat with alkali.
The alkali usually used is — sodium hydroxide.
As well as soap — glycerol is produced.
c) fat + sodium hydroxide → soap + glycerol
d) hydrolysis, fatty acids, sodium hydroxide.

Page 136 — Using Plant Oils

Q1 a) unsaturated
b) unsaturated
c) saturated
Q2 a) The substance in the first tube is a saturated fat.
b) i) The substances in the tube will go from orange to colourless. / The bromine water will be decolourised.
ii) An addition reaction takes place at the double bond of the unsaturated fat, forming a colourless dibromo compound.
Q3 a) Reaction with hydrogen with a nickel catalyst at about 60 °C.
b) Hydrogen reacts with the double-bonded carbons and opens out the double bonds.
Q4 Saturated fats as they can increase the amount of cholesterol in the blood, which can increase the risk of heart disease.

Page 137 — Detergents

Q1 a) false
b) true
c) false
d) true
e) true
f) false
Q2 a) hydrophilic ⬤〰〰〰 hydrophobic
b) The hydrophilic head forms intermolecular forces with water molecules. The hydrophobic tail forms intermolecular forces with oil molecules. So the detergent forms a coating around an oil droplet and lifts it away from the fabric.
Q3 a) i) Powder E
ii) Powders A and E — they don't work as well at higher temperatures because the enzymes have been denatured.
b) Any two from: e.g. it uses less energy. / It saves money on your energy bills. / You can wash more delicate clothes in the machine.

Pages 138-140 — Mixed Questions — Module C6

Q1 a) The electrons in an ionic solid are in a fixed position, so they can't move to conduct electricity.
b) i) At the cathode.
ii) $2I^- \rightarrow I_2 + 2e^- / 2I^- - 2e^- \rightarrow I_2$
c) The lead will displace the copper from the solution, giving a solution of lead chloride and solid copper.
Q2 a) Cathode — $O_2 + 4e^- + 2H_2O \rightarrow 4OH^-$
Anode — $2H_2 + 4OH^- \rightarrow 4H_2O + 4e^-$
b) Electrons are gained in the reaction at the cathode (reduction) and released by the reaction at the anode (oxidation).
c) E.g. they are more efficient. / They don't release pollutants. / There is a large amount of hydrogen available for use.
Q3 a) The paint coats the metal and prevents it from rusting.
b) Cutlery is made from stainless steel, which is a rustproof alloy of iron, carbon and chromium.
Q4 a) i) $Cu \rightarrow Cu^{2+} + 2e^-$
ii) $Cu^{2+} + 2e^- \rightarrow Cu$
b) i) 5 g
ii) 1.2 g forms in 30 minutes with 2 A,
so (1.2 ÷ 2) × 5 = 3 g forms in 30 minutes with 5 A,
so (30 ÷ 3) × 5 = **50 minutes** are required to form 5 g.
Q5 a) Ultraviolet light breaks the carbon-chlorine bonds in CFCs to form free radicals.
b) A ClO· free radical is produced when a Cl· free radical reacts with ozone. It reacts to regenerate the original Cl· free radical, so the reaction can repeat again and again.
c) i) They don't react with ozone.
ii) E.g. HFCs
Q6 a) E.g. it's a faster process. / The ethanol produced is much purer. / It has a higher atom economy. / You can recycle the reactants, so the total yield is higher.
b) Hydration requires much harsher reaction conditions so is a more expensive process to run.
Q7 a) B
b) A
c) River A contains sources of both permanent and temporary hardness. Once the temporary hardness was removed by boiling, less soap was needed to form a lasting lather.
Q8 a) Paul could add some bromine water to samples of each oil in test tubes and give them a shake. The unsaturated oil will decolourise the bromine water.
b) The unsaturated vegetable oil would be better for you, as saturated oils increase the amount of cholesterol in the blood and can cause heart disease.
c) E.g. making fuels/biodiesel / making soap / making paints / machine lubricants / detergents / cosmetics.

ISBN 978 1 84762 623 3

CRA44